MoSaic
God is here

Copyright © 2015 Scripture Union
First published 2015

ISBN 978 1 78506 220 9

Scripture Union
207–209 Queensway,
Bletchley,
Milton Keynes MK2 2EB
Email: info@scriptureunion.org.uk
Website: www.scriptureunion.org.uk

British Library
Cataloguing-in-Publication Data
A catalogue record for this book is available
from the British Library.

Original content from www.lightlive.org
Compiled by Maggie Barfield
Edited by Gemma Willis
Design by kwgraphicdesign
Printed in Malta by Gutenberg Press Ltd

Scripture quotations are from the
Contemporary English Version
(© American Bible Society, published by
HarperCollins*Publishers*) or from the
Good News Bible.

Scripture Union is an international
Christian charity working with churches in
more than 130 countries.

Prices quoted in this book are correct at
time of going to press.

Thank you for purchasing this book.
Any profits from this book support SU in
England and Wales to bring the good news
of Jesus Christ to children, young people
and families and to enable them to meet
God through the Bible and prayer.

Find out more about our work and how you
can get involved at:
www.scriptureunion.org.uk
(England and Wales)
www.suscotland.org.uk (Scotland)
www.suni.org (Northern Ireland)
www.scriptureunion.org (USA)
www.su.org.au (Australia)

Contents

What is Mosaic?

Scripture Union has been providing resources for people working with children in church settings for over sixty years.

As times have changed, so have the resources, of course. Where once 'Sunday School' was the highlight of the week for many children, today many other exciting activities compete with the events that churches provide. Where once school life was largely dull and mainly sedentary, today teachers have a vast range of ways of engaging children in the learning process. It is hard now for churches to 'compete' with all the opportunities and activities that fill the twenty-first-century child's life.

Yet Scripture Union still wants children to have the best resources to help them learn about God, decide to follow Jesus and grow in faith. This applies to children in churches both large and small, as well as those who have no contact with churches. We publish a range of resources to equip children's workers, whatever their situation. This includes the *Light* range, which has resources for different age groups from 3 to 14.

You told us...

You have only a few children in your group and you have a wide age range. Maybe there are a 3-year-old, two 7-year-olds, a 10-year-old boy and a couple of girls who will soon be 14. Buying the whole range of *Light* products would be much too expensive and it would be time-consuming to go through each product looking for suitable activities for your session each week. You need a flexible printed product which enables you to choose suitable activities that will work across the age group.

Settings where *Mosaic* works best...

■ Many churches begin Sunday worship with all ages together. In other churches, everyone arrives together, but separate into adult and children's groups and meet together again for a final time of worship. *Mosaic* can be used in either of these scenarios when the number of children attending is too small to make the provision of separate age groups practical.

■ *Mosaic* could be used where the premises in which children meet are limited so that it is impossible to provide more than one group.

■ *Mosaic* would also be useful where there are few adults able to work with the children. (Of course, there should, for reasons of safety and child protection, always be at least two adults with CRB clearance with the children.) In this case, most of the activities can be done together, with separate, targeted activities for younger and older children later in the session.

■ *Mosaic* is ideal if you are starting a new children's group and want a simple programme to work with.

How to run a *Mosaic* session

WHAT YOU GET

Mosaic is a flexible resource designed to give you a structured programme.

There are also extra ideas which you can add to suit the time you have available and the group you are leading. Some of the extra resources can be downloaded from the *LightLive* website at www.lightlive.org. But even if you cannot access the website, this book provides all you need for 12 exciting and meaningful sessions.

Introduction
Each series of two to five sessions begins with essential Bible background to the passages you will be using with the children. There is also an important paragraph giving insights into how the series can be tailored to the children in your group.

Core programme
Four activities are provided as the basic template for each session – a way of exploring the Bible, a worship response, and two options which help the group apply the Bible teaching to their own lives.

Extension ideas
Three extension ideas are suggested to provide more targeted activities for younger children (perhaps under-8s) and more challenging things for older children to do (perhaps those aged 10 and over). Obviously, abilities differ and you will have to direct individual children to the activities best suited to them. Fresh ideas are suggested for each session for the series 'Learn and remember' verse.

Case studies
Advice designed to inspire and encourage you in your work – from a writer experienced in working with small churches.

Tips
Helpful advice for working with your mixed-age group can be found in the *Mosaic* clinic.

LightLive
Create a group on *LightLive* online (www.lightlive.org) and you will have access to a huge choice of resources for your group. The database is searchable by topic and Bible passage so that you will never be short of an idea for your group-time or special event!

Helpful resources
Look on page 96 for targeted recommendations of other Scripture Union titles which will supplement your programmes, provide ideas to help your group grow in faith and help you increase your confidence.

Every week online
You can enhance your weekly sessions with downloads including:
- 'Bible story picture': a regular activity for 2–7s (These are also available as photocopiable pages at the end of each session.)
- 'Audio Bible story': a regular audio Bible story for 3–7s
- 'Learn and remember': a PowerPoint of a Bible verse to learn, for 5–11s
- 'Presentation': an activity with animation for 11–14s

SERIES INTRODUCTION

JEREMIAH THE PROPHET

The lordship and foreknowledge of God are explored through key experiences in the life of his prophet, Jeremiah.

BIBLE BACKGROUND FOR YOU

Jeremiah lived and worked in the years before the fall of Jerusalem in 587 BC.

These were difficult years for Judah. Apart from the brief respite during the reign of Josiah (2 Kings 22,23), the kings were weak and self-serving. The Babylonian armies were at the door, social order was crumbling, the economic situation deteriorating, justice perverted and God ignored. We might feel that there are certain parallels with our own times. In calling the people back to God and warning of dire consequences if they did not change, Jeremiah faced constant opposition; the burning of the scroll (Jeremiah 36:20–26) and being placed in the cistern or well (Jeremiah 38:1–13) are two examples.

But his determination remained strong. He knew that God was in control, as the story of the potter shows (Jeremiah 18:1–12). And as the world fell apart around him he pointed to hope for the future (Jeremiah 31:1–6), not just by speaking of a return from exile but by buying a field (Jeremiah 32:1–15). In the face of our own circumstances, how do we give practical recognition to the fact that God is in control of world events and our own lives? In the face of political and economic uncertainties, how do we show a strong hope for the future, knowing that God is the King of kings?

For your small group with a wide age range

Through the story of Jeremiah, this series demonstrates that God is Lord and knows everything – about us and about the past, present and future. That is why it is right to trust him, even when being a Christian seems hard. Within your small group, there may be a wide range of experience and maturity. Some will trust God easily and readily, while others are finding the way difficult.

Try to encourage everyone to follow Jeremiah's example of honesty, courage and hope. If particular activities are too hard for some, encourage others in the group to support them, for instance by writing or reading for them.

Resources for ministry

Bitesize Bible Songs and *Bitesize Bible Songs 2* are audio CD collections of chart-sound songs featuring Bible verses for children to memorise. (Songs are also available as mp3 files, as albums or single tracks.) With catchy music and mini-activities to provide creative and fun ways of applying the verses into everyday life, these songs will help get God's word stuck in your heads!

Highlights from *LightLive*

Go to the 'Search *LightLive*' tab at www.lightlive.org and enter this session's Bible reference to find:

- 'Audio Bible story': a regular mp3 download for 3–7s
- 'Learn and remember': a PowerPoint of a Bible verse to learn, for 5–11s (see also page 35)
- 'Presentation': an activity with animation for 11–14s

SESSION 1
In the potter's shop

Bible:
Jeremiah 18:1–12

Aim: To realise that God knows everything and wants us to change

CORE PROGRAMME

For 3 to 14s

Bible story - All change

 minutes

Why: to realise that God knows everything and wants us to change
With: SU *Bible Timeline* or the *Big Bible Storybook Timeline* (optional, see page 96 for details)

1 Acting
Look at the *Timeline* (or an illustrated Bible) together. Give the children a few minutes to see if they can identify someone who changed their life and turned to God. Then ask them to act it out for the group so that they can guess who it is. (If they need help you could start by acting out Saul on the road to Damascus.)

2 All change game
Explain to the children that you are going to read a story and they have to listen very carefully. Invite each child to find a partner, asking one to go to one end of the room, while the other stands opposite

them. Explain that when they hear the word 'change' or 'changed' both children must run to the other side of the room, giving their partner a 'high five' (a hand slap in the air!) as they run past them. As they pass, they shout, 'All change!'

Read the account here, remembering to pause while the children exchange places. If there's an odd child out, invite that child to join another pair and run with them. If you have no room to run about, you could ask them to swap chairs or jump up instead.

'Hello, this is Jeremiah. I am a prophet and God gives me special messages to pass on to people. The other day God told me to go to the pottery. He said that when I got there he would tell me what to say to the people. So I went there and saw the potter making clay pots on his pottery wheel. I noticed that whenever the clay would not take the shape he wanted, he would **change** his mind and form it into some other shape. I saw him **change** his mind over and over again. Each time the clay **changed** shape, he formed another pot. He was very clever. As the potter **changed** his clay, God showed me what he wanted to say.

'This is God's message: "I have power over you, just as a potter has power over clay. I am going to destroy you and your country because you have **changed** from your good ways into bad ways. But if you decide to **change** back to your good ways, I will **change** my mind, and not destroy you. If I promise to make you strong, but then you **change** and start doing bad things again, I will **change** my mind and not help you. I have decided to strike you and your country with disaster, and I won't **change** my mind unless you stop doing bad things and start loving me again! You need to **change** your ways and start living good lives. But I know you won't listen. You might as well answer, 'We don't care what you say. We are not going to **change**. We have made plans to do very bad things, and we are going to be stubborn and do what we want!'"'

3 Counting
Read the story a second time, challenging the children to count how many times you say 'change' or 'changed'. (*There are 12.*)

4 Reflect
Say that the people were reminded so many times in the story to 'change' their ways. Ask the children what they think God was trying to tell his people. God knows everything and is always giving us opportunities to change. Pray together and ask God to help us to listen to him, and put right the things in our lives that he

wants us to change.
CORE PROGRAMME CONTINUED

Play dough

 minutes

Why: to ask God to show us where we need to change
With: recipe for play dough

1 Be aware of allergies before you start. Sit in a circle and hold up a blob of play dough. Ask the children what they have learned about God today. Pass the blob around and ask each child to change its shape. (With a large group, have several pieces of dough going round.)

2 While they are doing this, ask the children how we know what changes to make in our lives. Explain that as we listen to God and talk to him and read the Bible, God will show us things that we need to change in our lives that will help us to love him more.

3 Pass round more dough, so everyone is holding some. Ask the children to pray silently as they continue to mould, shape and change the play dough.

PHOTOCOPIABLE PART
For use with **Play dough**

RECIPE

Play dough

1 To make the dough, take two cups of plain cooking flour, one cup of salt, one cup of water and two tablespoons of cooking oil. You could add food colouring to make the dough a more interesting colour.

2 Mix all the ingredients together and keep in a cool place and covered in a plastic food bag or carrier bag until required.

(Don't make this too far in advance as it could go off!)

Praise shout

 **minutes**

Why: to praise God for knowing all about us and still loving us
With: 'Shout it out' sheets from page 9 (optional)

1 Explain that in the story of Jeremiah we see that God is like the potter who knows all about everything that he makes. He knows everything about them and he still loves them.

2 Invite the children to use their own ideas to fill in the gaps on a copy of the 'Shout it out' sheet (page 9). Alternatively, challenge them to complete the sentence: 'You know [*idea*] and you still love us.'

3 Use their ideas in a praise shout.

    Caller: You know everything about us and you still love us.
    All: We praise you, God!
    Caller: You know [*idea*] and you still love us.
    All: We praise you, God!

Encourage the children to take turns to be the 'caller', and keep going until they run out of ideas.

Identity game

 **minutes**

Why: to remember that God knows all about us

1 Ask the children each to think of and write down (with help for early learners) one thing that the rest of the group doesn't know about them.

2 Collect and shuffle the slips of paper, then read each one out loud and challenge the children to identify who it is about.

3 Encourage the children to think of one person who knows most things about them. Does that person know everything about them? If not, who does?

4 Say that in today's Bible verses they are going to discover that God knows everything about us.

Sheet for use with **Praise shout**

SHOUT iT OUT!

Fill in the gaps with your own ideas. Then use this as a praise shout.

caller: You know everything about us and you still love us.

All: we praise you, God!

caller: You know

and you still love us.

All: we praise you, God!

caller: You know

and you still love us

All: we praise you, God!

caller: You know

and you still love us

All: we praise you, God!

caller: You know

and you still love us.

All: we praise you, God!

caller: You know

and you still love us.

All: we praise you, God!

EXTENSION IDEAS

Activities for younger children

Game

(10) *minutes*

Why: to get to know Jeremiah
With: SU *Bible Timeline* or the *Big Bible Storybook Timeline*

1 Find where Jeremiah appears on the *Timeline*. Explain that Jeremiah keeps telling God's people in Jerusalem to change because they are always doing bad things, but they won't listen.

2 Choose one child to represent 'Jeremiah', and stand them facing the wall. Encourage the other children to pretend to be the people doing bad things, and stand with their backs turned to 'Jeremiah'. Ask 'Jeremiah' to turn around suddenly and shout, 'God says to change your ways.' Everyone freezes. Whoever 'Jeremiah' sees moving is out!

Bible story picture

(5) - (10) *minutes*

Why: to realise that God wants us to be close to him
With: a copy of the picture on page 11 (printed on A4 paper) for each child or enlarged copies for group use, art and craft materials

1 You can use the picture as an introduction to the Bible story or to help you review the story together.

2 Ask the children to describe what they can see on the Bible story picture. What do they think the man sitting down is doing? (*Making pots.*) Use the words 'potter' and 'pottery' to help the children develop their understanding.

3 Introduce the other person in the picture as Jeremiah, one of God's friends and messengers. Say that God told Jeremiah to go and watch the potter making his pots.

For older children

Matching activity

(5) - (10) *minutes*

Why: to learn about prophets in the Bible
With: page 12, SU *Bible Timeline* or the *Big Bible Storybook Timeline* (optional, see page 96 for details)

1 Ask the children what they think a prophet does. Consider various answers and establish that a prophet is someone who passes on messages that God gives them.

2 Challenge the children to name some prophets. Encourage them to use their Bibles or the *Bible Timeline*. See who can find the most.

3 To discover some more about prophets, encourage the children to work in pairs or small groups to find the Bible verses from page 12. By doing this they should be able to link the verses with the prophets.

THE LEARN AND REMEMBER VERSE

'Even before I speak, you already know what I will say.'

Psalm 139:4

Play a game of Hangman with the verse. Leave a dash for each consonant and challenge the children to guess the words as a letter is revealed.

When you have completed the verse, say it together several times to help them remember it.

Find a poster for this Learn and remember verse on page 35.

You could also use the song 'Even before I speak', on the *Bitesize Bible Songs 2* CD, available from Scripture Union.

Use with **Bible story picture**
The potter's house Jeremiah 18:1–12

For use with **Matching activity**

Who's the prophet?

Read these Bible verses. (You can use the contents page to find the more unusual Bible books.) Each verse will help you draw a line between the statements below and the name of the prophet who said it.

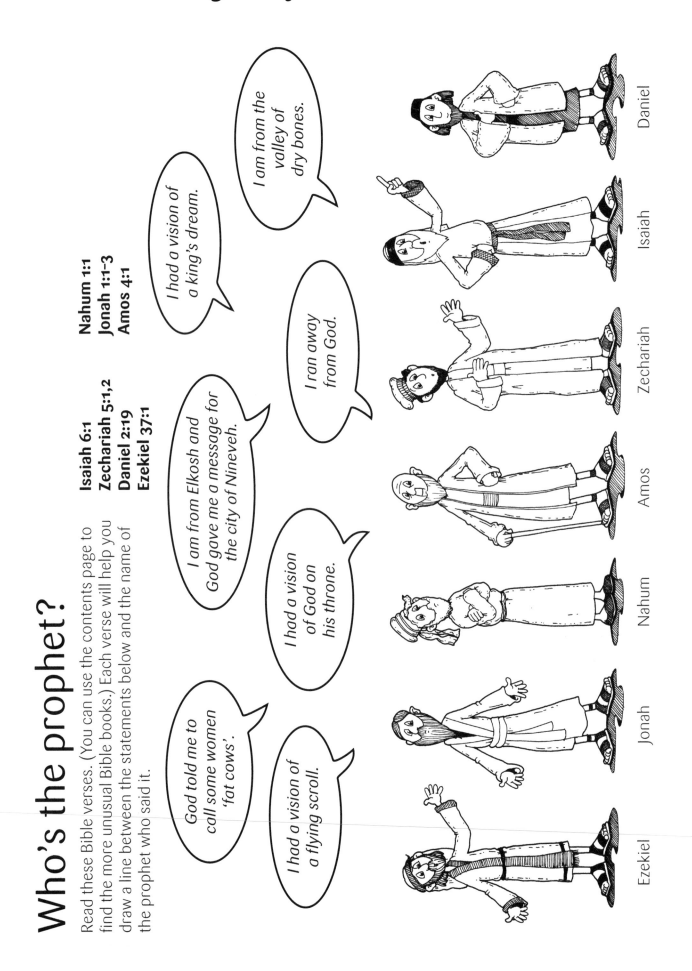

Nahum 1:1
Jonah 1:1-3
Amos 4:1

Isaiah 6:1
Zechariah 5:1,2
Daniel 2:19
Ezekiel 37:1

I am from the valley of dry bones.

I had a vision of a king's dream.

I ran away from God.

I am from Elkosh and God gave me a message for the city of Nineveh.

I had a vision of God on his throne.

God told me to call some women 'fat cows'.

I had a vision of a flying scroll.

Daniel

Isaiah

Zechariah

Amos

Nahum

Jonah

Ezekiel

SESSION 2

Buying a field

Bible:
Jeremiah 31:1–6; 32:1–15

Aim: To live in hope because God knows the future

CORE PROGRAMME

For 3 to 14s

Bible story sketch

(15) *minutes*

Why: to live in hope because God knows the future
With: SU *Bible Timeline* or the *Big Bible Storybook Timeline* (see page 96 for details), copies of the script given on page 14 (all optional)

1 *Bible Timeline*
Challenge the children to use the *Bible Timeline* to find different people whose story involved land. Let them take it in turns to suggest someone and explain how their story involved land. For example, God sent Abraham to a new land. Say that today we will hear how everyone is amazed when Jeremiah decides to buy a field in an undesirable location.

2 Sketch
Ask two leaders, or a leader and a child, to practise and perform the sketch between Jerry (Jeremiah) and Gazump, a friendly estate agent using the script on page 14.

3 Review
Invent actions for the words 'trust', 'future', 'faith' and 'hope'. Say, with everyone doing the actions:

'The present time looked bleak with an enemy army poised to destroy the city, but Jeremiah continued to **trust** God for the **future**. Jeremiah was able to do this because he had **faith** in God.

'When Jeremiah bought the field, he showed everyone that, because he had **faith** in God, he had **hope** for the **future**. He **trusted** that God would restore the city.

'We can have **hope** if we have **faith** in God and trust him for our **future**.'

Trust in God

(10) – (30) *minutes*

Why: to remember to trust in God
With: musical instruments (optional)

1 Discuss with your group all the different things they or their friends could be worried about. Write them on sticky notes or a large sheet of paper.

2 Encourage the children to create a song or rap to help them and their friends to trust in God when faced with these situations. They could do this with or without instruments. If appropriate you might want to talk with the children about why trusting in God may sometimes be a

challenge – but encourage them that with God's help it is possible!

3 Practise until everyone is confident with the words and rhythm. Show your song or rap to another children's group (or the whole church family) and encourage them to trust in God, as Jeremiah did.

Daily calendar

(10) – (15) *minutes*

Why: to thank God because he knows our future
With: calendar template and instructions for 'Daily calendar' (page 15)

1 Help the children to make a 'Daily calendar' (page 15).

2 Invite the children to move the day marker to 'today', and help them choose something that happened yesterday to draw or write in the space for that day.

3 Invite them to say the prayer written on the day marker, adding to the line, 'Thank you, God, for yesterday when...' with the events they have drawn or written. Remind the children that God knew what would happen yesterday before it happened, and he knows what will happen tomorrow.

4 Encourage the children to take their calendar home and use it in the same way each day.

Script for use with **Bible story sketch**

CHARACTERS
Jerry: Jeremiah – prophet and palace prisoner, he has a ball and chain attached to his ankle.
Gazump: An efficient and friendly estate agent.

SCENE
The office of Diddle and Gazump, estate agents.

Jerry: Good morning, is this the office of Diddle and Gazump, estate agents?

Gazump: It most certainly is. What kind of property are you looking for?

Jerry: Well, actually, I'm looking for a field.

Gazump: Right, well, let me just take some details. What is your current address?

Jerry: The palace courtyard.

Gazump: I see. Are you a royal servant?

Jerry: Err... No... More of a royal prisoner!

Gazump: Mmmm! I guess that would account for the ball and chain. And what kind of field are you looking for?

Jerry: There's a field in Anathoth that belongs to my cousin, Hanamel. He said that he's quite happy to sell it to me for 17 pieces of silver.

Gazump: I'm sure he is! I expect he can't get out of there fast enough.

Jerry: Sorry?

Gazump: Don't you realise that the Babylonian army is about to invade the whole city? Once they've captured the people and their land all our houses and fields will be quite worthless. First, you'll lose your 17 silver coins to Hanamel and then you'll lose your field.

Jerry: Ye-es, but one day the city will belong to us again.

Gazump: You reckon?

Jerry: Absolutely! God has promised to restore Jerusalem to us. That's why I'm buying the field: to show everyone that I trust God and believe that he will give the city back to us one day.

Gazump: I see. It's a kind of investment then.

Jerry: Spot on! An investment in the future!

Gazump: And what exactly do you want me to do?

Jerry: I'd like you to draw up the contracts. I intend to give everything to my friend, Baruch, who will ensure that it's all kept in a safe place.

Gazump: Nowhere is safe in these troubled times.

Jerry: That's OK. God has told me to tell Baruch that the paperwork will be quite safe in a clay jar.

Gazump: Yes, I've heard that there's a safe place for scrolls in clay jars down by the Dead Sea. Hopefully Baruch will find somewhere equally safe. Drop by my office in a few days, along with Hanamel, and you can both sign the contract of sale.

Jerry: Great! See you then.

Template for use with **Daily calendar**

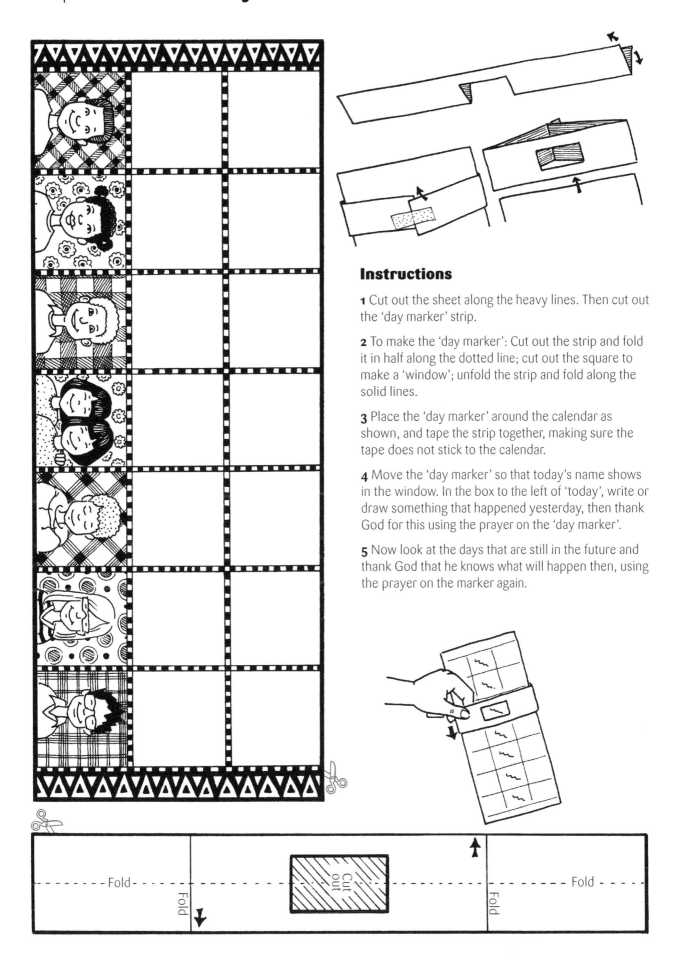

Instructions

1 Cut out the sheet along the heavy lines. Then cut out the 'day marker' strip.

2 To make the 'day marker': Cut out the strip and fold it in half along the dotted line; cut out the square to make a 'window'; unfold the strip and fold along the solid lines.

3 Place the 'day marker' around the calendar as shown, and tape the strip together, making sure the tape does not stick to the calendar.

4 Move the 'day marker' so that today's name shows in the window. In the box to the left of 'today', write or draw something that happened yesterday, then thank God for this using the prayer on the 'day marker'.

5 Now look at the days that are still in the future and thank God that he knows what will happen then, using the prayer on the marker again.

CORE PROGRAMME CONTINUED

Growing seeds

 minutes

Why: to create a reminder that God gives us hope
With: cress or alfalfa seeds, polystyrene food trays (or similar), paper kitchen towel, templates from page 17 (optional)

1 Help each child cut out letters 'H' 'O' 'P' 'E' 6–10 cm high from kitchen towel (templates are on page 17).

2 Invite the children to lay out the letters on trays and add a few drops of water. Encourage them to carefully sprinkle seeds on the damp paper. Let the children take the trays home to water and watch the letters grow.

3 Say that Jeremiah bought a field as a reminder that, one day, peaceful activities like farming and harvesting would be part of life in Jerusalem again. He lived in hope because he trusted God – and we can do the same!

EXTENSION IDEAS

Activities for younger children

Poster

 minutes

Why: to know that we can trust God
With: sheets of paper, crayons, a large sheet of paper, glue

1 Tell the children that Jeremiah and his people were worried and sad when they had to leave their land, but they trusted that God would look after them. They knew he would keep his promises to them.

2 Tell the children that we can trust God too, however we feel. Talk with them about times when they feel happy (or sad, frightened, excited or lonely). Emphasise that they can trust God in all these times.

3 Ask the children to draw pictures of children who are happy, sad, excited or frightened. (These do not need to be of the children

themselves.) Ask the children to tell you about their pictures and label their pictures to show this.

4 Stick all the pictures on to a larger background sheet. Label your poster: 'We can all trust God.'

Bible story picture

 minutes

Why: to learn to trust God
With: a copy of the picture on page 18 (printed on A4 paper) for each child or enlarged copies for group use, art and craft materials

1 You can use the picture as an introduction to the Bible story or to help you review the story together.

2 On the blank side of the Bible story picture, ask the children to imagine they have a field and draw what they would do with it. They may cover it with green grass, keep cows, grow plants, play – anything they like.

3 Turn the paper over and find a picture of Jeremiah with the field he bought. When he bought it, he knew he could not keep cows or grow flowers or play in it (list the things the children have drawn in their fields), maybe for a long time. But he knew that, one day, he would be able to – because God had told him so, and he knew he could trust what God said.

For older children

Re-enactment

 minutes

Why: to know that we can live with hope because of God's knowledge and power
With: sheet of flip-chart paper with 'Jerusalem' written at the top, copies of pages 19 and 20 with the pictures cut out in advance, Bibles

1 Put the flip-chart paper on the floor and ask the young people to imagine that this sheet is a map of Jerusalem. Explain that we are going to lay out on the map the situation that Jeremiah was facing in today's Bible story, to help us understand what things were like for him.

2 Hand out the pictures from page 19 so that everyone has at least one (but keep the script for your use). Explain that you are going to read out a summary of today's Bible passage and that each person should place (and remove) their picture on the paper at the point in the story where it is mentioned.

3 Read out the summary from page 20. You may want to stop halfway through the story and ask the young people how they would have felt if they had been stuck in prison in the middle of Jerusalem at the time the soldiers were surrounding it. Then continue to read out the Bible summary.

4 When you have finished, ask the young people why they think Jeremiah bought a field in the middle of a siege. What was this a sign of? Get two volunteers to read Jeremiah 32:1–15 and Jeremiah 31:1–6.

5 Make the point that, if we are living to please God, God promises that, although things may be hard and seem hopeless at times, ultimately he will bring good things to those who trust him (Revelation 21:3–5).

THE LEARN AND REMEMBER VERSE

'Even before I speak, you already know what I will say.'

Psalm 139:4

Read the words aloud together, with the following actions: 'Even before I (point to self) speak (chatty hand) you (point up) already know (index finger to head) what I (point to self) will say (chatty hand).'

Repeat three times using the actions, then try to say it again using the actions in place of the words.

Find a poster for this Learn and remember verse on page 35.

You could also use the song 'Even before I speak', on the *Bitesize Bible Songs 2* CD, available from Scripture Union.

Templates for use with **Growing seeds**

Use with **Bible story picture**
Jeremiah buys a field Jeremiah 31:1–6; 32:1–15

Summary and pictures for use with **Re-enactment**

BATTLE RE-ENACTMENT
Give out the pictures. Read out the following script and get the young people to carry out the actions that are described in italics.

So, this is the scene: Jez is having a seriously bad day. There he is, sitting in the middle of Jerusalem. *(The young person who has the picture of Jeremiah should put it in the middle of the paper.)* There are houses all around him. *(The young people who have the pictures of the houses should scatter them around where Jeremiah is.)* The next thing he knows, the king throws him in the prison in the middle of Jerusalem. *(The prison picture should be put in the middle of piece of paper and Jeremiah on top of it.)* His crime? Telling people what God is saying. This is not a good day.

Just when we think things couldn't get any worse, our mate Jez remembers that being in prison isn't his only problem.

The city is surrounded by Babylonian soldiers. *(The pictures of soldiers should be placed on the paper so they surround all the houses in Jerusalem.)* They stretch all the way around the city, and at any moment they are going to invade. There is no way for anyone to get out – the city and everyone in it seem doomed.

Then, in the middle of all this, God tells Jez to do something that seems really… well… er… odd. God tells Jez to buy a field in Jerusalem. *(The picture of the flower should be placed in the Jerusalem area – inside the area surrounded by the soldiers.)* So that's exactly what he does. While he's in prison in a city that's surrounded by an army about to rip it to shreds, Jez buys a field in the city.

This is the reason why: Jez says, 'God has told me, "Things are going to be tough. This city is going to be invaded by the army

(move the soldiers inwards on the paper) and loads of houses will be destroyed. *(Rip up the houses.)* But I have told Jez to buy a field as a way of showing you that even though many houses will be destroyed and loads of people will be killed, this is still a place worth investing in. There is hope for this city. *(Remove the soldiers and the prison to only Jeremiah and the flower remain.)* One day people will want to buy the land here again. Though times are tough now, things will get better."'

Soldiers

Pictures for use with **Re-enactment**

Jeremiah

Houses

Sunflower

Prison

SESSION 3

Burning a scroll

Bible:
Jeremiah 36

Aim: To discover that God's Word can't be stopped

CORE PROGRAMME

For 3 to 14s

Make scrolls

⑤ – ⑩ *minutes*

Why: to set the scene for the Bible story
With: lining paper, sticks (perhaps wooden kebab skewers), used teabags, water

1 Give each child a length of lining paper (about the size of an A3 sheet of paper) to create a scroll with. Get them to tear it along the sides and paint it using a teabag dipped in warm water to make it look old.

2 Encourage them to use glue or sticky tape to attach a stick to each end, then leave them to dry. These can be used in 'Bible story with drama' (but not put through the shredder, unless the children are happy to have their work chopped up!).

Bible story with drama

⑳ – ㉕ *minutes*

Why: to discover that God's Word can't be stopped
With: SU *Bible Timeline* or the *Big Bible Storybook Timeline* (see page 96 for details), Jeremiah's script from page 22, scrolls from page 23, a paper shredder, flame-coloured paper, a simple headdress to represent Jeremiah, a crown, *Bitesize Bible Songs* or *Bitesize Bible Songs 2* (both optional) and means to play them

1 Act the story

In advance, make four signs for the room: 'Jeremiah's House', 'The Temple', 'The Palace' and 'The King's Room'. Disguise the shredder with flame-coloured paper if possible. Explain that you are going to be Jeremiah and the children are going to be other characters. Begin in 'Jeremiah's House'. If you are not able to move around your room, get the children to hold up the appropriate place labels during the story.

Put on the Jeremiah headdress and follow the script from page 22, putting the scrolls in the 'fire' when the story tells you to do so. It would be good if you could tell the story from memory!

2 *Bible Timeline*

If you do not have an SU *Bible Timeline*, follow the suggestions below, showing the children the relevant parts in the Bible (*Ezra, a Gospel, Acts*).

Ask the children to find Jeremiah's name on the *Bible Timeline*. Give them one of the scrolls and get them to lay it beside the *Timeline*. Say that God's message could not be stopped, even when the king burned it up!

Read the message on the scroll, with the children. Ask a child to move the scroll so that it is near the picture of Ezra and say that Ezra lived about 100 years after Jeremiah. Say that God's message was still being given to the people.

Now ask another child to move the scroll near to the picture of Jesus, the teacher. Explain that 400 years later, Jesus brought God's message to the people.

Invite another child to move the scroll to the picture 'The Holy Spirit sends'. Tell them that Paul and others continued to spread God's message with people willing to listen.

Encourage another child to move the scroll to the end of the *Timeline*, and say that God's message is still being told today.

Read the scroll again together. Reinforce again that God's Word cannot be stopped!

Script for use with **Bible story with drama**

(Start at the 'Jeremiah's House' sign.)

Jeremiah: Hello, I'm Jeremiah and God gives me messages for the people. Do you remember hearing about when I visited the potter and bought a field?
Well, the king and his people have not been listening to me. They are ignoring God's message and think that they know what's best! So God has given me another message and this time I have to write it down on a scroll.

(Ask one child to be Baruch and to pretend to write God's message on the scroll as you dictate it.)

Jeremiah: God says, 'I want you to stop doing wrong things. If you say sorry and change your ways then I will forgive you.' The king thinks I'm a troublemaker and doesn't believe I'm giving him God's message so I'm banned from the Temple. *(Turn to Baruch.)* Baruch, you must take this scroll and, when all the people are meeting there, I want you to read it out loud.

(Move to the 'The Temple' sign and ask the children to act as the people while the person acting as Baruch pretends to read the scroll.)

Jeremiah: Can you remember what the message was that Baruch read out?
One of the men who heard the message went off to the palace and told the king's officials what Baruch had said. They immediately sent for Baruch and asked him to read the scroll to them.

(Move to the 'The Palace' sign. The children are now acting as the king's officials while Baruch reads the scroll.)

Jeremiah: When the officials heard that I had told Baruch what to write they said that Baruch and I were in great danger and we should go somewhere safe to hide. Then they went to see the king.

(Move to the 'The King's Room sign' and ask one of the children to be King Jehoiakim and the others to be his servants.)

Jeremiah: It was winter time and the king was sitting huddled beside a fire to keep warm. When the officials told him about the scroll he sent Jehudi to get it and read it to him.

(Ask a child to be Jehudi and see if the children can remember what the message was.)

Jeremiah: You'll never believe what the king did next! He started cutting pieces off the scroll and throwing them into the fire! The officials begged the king to stop but he paid no attention. Then he sent his son and some friends to search for Baruch and me, but God kept us safe.

(Invite the children take turns to cut a piece off the scroll and give them to another adult present to feed into the shredder.)

Jeremiah: They thought that nobody would be able to hear God's message now! But God is much cleverer than any king! He told me to get another scroll and write down everything that had been on the first one.

(Ask Baruch to write another message on the scroll, getting the children to remind you what it was.)

Jeremiah: Then God told me to add an extra message. God said, 'King Jehoiakim, not only have you burned Jeremiah's scroll, you will not believe that my message is true. I am very angry with you and you will be punished.' So you see that no matter what happened, God's message still kept going – it could never be stopped!

Scrolls for use with **Bible story with drama**

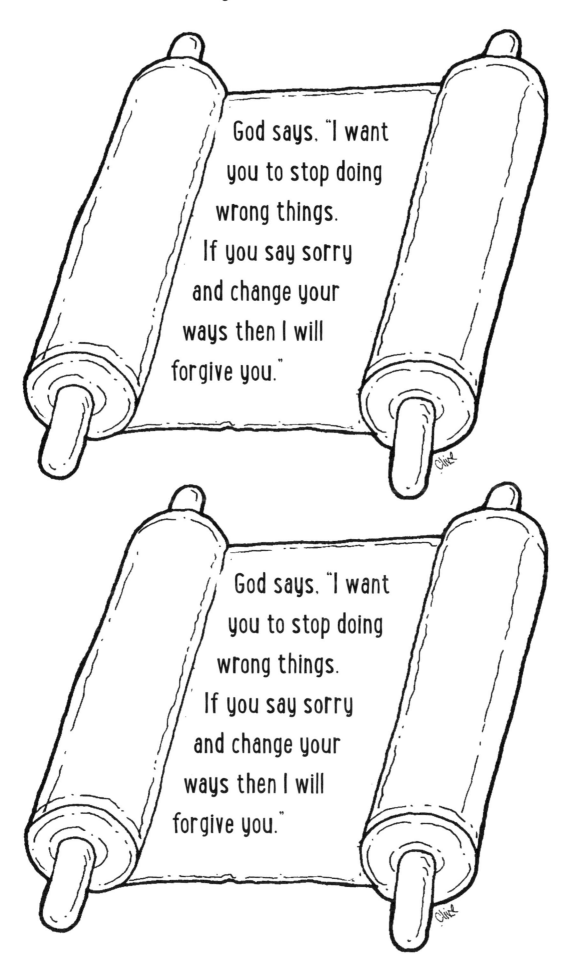

CORE PROGRAMME CONTINUED

3 Think about

Remember to emphasise that God's love is unconditional and that our relationship with God is not simply based on being 'good' or 'doing the right thing'. Remind the children that when God uses Jeremiah to ask the people to change their ways, it is because he loves the people and wants what is best for them.

4 Sing and pray

Play the song 'Come back' from Joel 2:13b (*Bitesize Bible Songs* CD) or 'Call to me' from Jeremiah 33:3 (*Bitesize Bible Songs 2* CD), available as individual track downloads from www. scriptureunion.org.uk/music. This is the message that God gave to Jeremiah and is still his message to us today. Ask the children to say their own quiet thank-you prayer to God that his Word cannot be stopped.

Game
⑤ - ⑩ *minutes*

Why: to enjoy God's Word
With: *Bitesize Bible Songs* CD or a recording of Bible words being read to music, means to play them

1 Play a form of musical statues using lively tracks from the *Bitesize Bible Songs* CD while the children dance and sing along with the songs. Alternatively, play the recording of Bible verses being read to music.

2 Tell the children that when the music stops, they should stop moving around and start to march on the spot, shouting, 'God's Word can't be stopped!' If you see any child dancing after the music has stopped, ask them to sit down. If you are using the songs, then ask the children sitting to clap (or wave) while the music is being played.

3 Continue the game until you're left with one child.

4 Sing a song together. Then shout, 'God's Word can't be stopped!'

Finding out
⑩ - ⑮ *minutes*

Why: to discover that God's Word keeps on going
With: fact sheets for 'Finding out' (enlarge and copy from pages 25, 26 and 27)

1 Lay the fact sheets in a line on the floor, leaving enough room for the children to jump between them.

2 Read the first fact about the Bible aloud: 'About 1000 BC God's Word was written on scrolls and read to the people in the Temple.' Ask everyone to join in and say the last sentence together: 'God's Word could not be stopped!' (This is repeated at the end of each fact sheet.) For a shorter game, use facts 1, 2, 3, 4, 6 and 10.

3 Tell the children to jump forward after reading each fact. When you reach the end, chat about ways your church is keeping God's Word alive. Pray for those people involved.

4 Older children might enjoy finding out more about some of the people and organisations mentioned.

Fact sheets 1 to 4 for use with **Finding out**

FACT 1

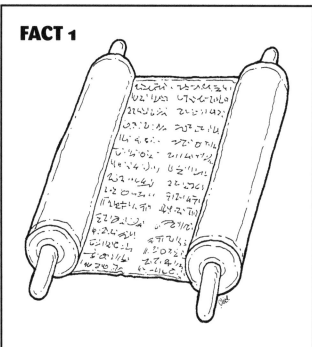

About 1000 BC
God's Word was written on scrolls and read to the people in the Temple. God's Word could not be stopped!

FACT 2

About 500 BC
God's messages to prophets, including Jeremiah, were written down and read to the kings and the people. God's Word could not be stopped!

FACT 3

About AD 30
Jesus brought God's message to the people. He was God's Word in human form! God's Word could not be stopped!

FACT 4

About AD 60
Peter and Paul and others wrote down God's message in books and letters for God's people to read. God's Word could not be stopped!

Fact sheets 5 to 8 for use with **Finding out**

FACT 5

About AD 450
The Bible was translated into Latin so that more people could understand it. God's Word could not be stopped!

FACT 6

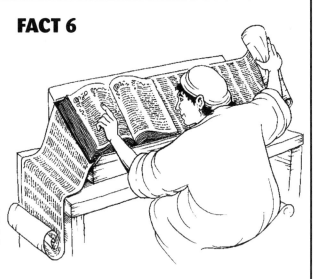

About 1526
William Tyndale translated the New Testament from Greek into English so that more people could understand it.

Some people thought this was wrong and had Tyndale killed but his Bible was still there. God's Word could not be stopped!

FACT 7

About 1800
A young Welsh girl, called Mary Jones, so wanted a Bible of her own that she worked for six years to save enough money to buy one. She then walked 25 miles barefoot to the home of a minister who she knew had some Welsh Bibles for sale. When she arrived there were none left but the Rev Thomas Charles was so sorry for her that he gave her his own Bible. God's Word cannot be stopped!

When other people heard this story, the British and Foreign Bible Society was formed to enable more people to own the Bible in their own language. God's Word cannot be stopped!

FACT 8

About 1834
By the time he died, William Carey had translated the Bible into at least 44 different Indian languages and dialects so that people in India could read the Bible. God's Word cannot be stopped!

Fact sheets 9 and 10 for use with **Finding out**

FACT 9

About 1930

William Cameron Townsend went to Guatemala to give Spanish Bibles to the people there, but one of them said, 'If your God is so great, why doesn't he speak in my language?', so he started to translate the Bible into their language. This was the start of the Wycliffe Bible Translators, which works very hard to provide Bibles in every language spoken on earth. God's Word cannot be stopped!

FACT 10

Today

People from many organisations like the British and Foreign Bible Society, Wycliffe Bible Translators, Scripture Union and your church work hard to make sure that as many people as possible are able to read God's Word in the Bible. God's Word cannot be stopped!

For more information see:
www.christianheroes.com
www.wycliffe.org.uk
www.scottishbiblesociety.org/projects
www.biblesociety.org.uk
www.scriptureunion.org.uk

Cards for use with **Read the Bible**

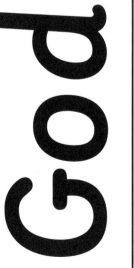

God God God God

EXTENSION IDEAS

Activities for younger children

Read the Bible

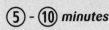 *minutes*

Why: to begin to read God's words in the Bible
With: cards with the word 'God' written on them (enlarge and copy from page 27 or write out, freehand), *The Big Bible Storybook*, any Bibles with fairly large print

1 Let the children open the Bibles and turn the pages, looking at the patterns of the words.

2 Give each child a card and read it. Point out the round 'o' in the middle and the distinctive shapes of the other two letters.

3 Try to find the word 'God' on the Bible pages. Continue searching for as long as the children are interested.

4 Comment that you have found the name 'God' many times in the Bible. Why is that? It is because the Bible is God's book and tells us all about him.

5 Pray together, pointing at the cards and saying the word each time you reach the name 'God': 'Loving God, thank you for your book, the Bible. We hear about God, learn about God and find out what God wants us to do. The Bible is your book and it's our book, loving God.'

Bible story picture

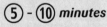 *minutes*

Why: to discover that what God says is important
With: a copy of the picture on page 29 (printed on A4 paper) for each child or enlarged copies for group use, art and craft materials

1 You can use the picture as an introduction to the Bible story or to help you review the story together.

2 Point to the figure of Jeremiah on the Bible story picture. The children may remember him from previous sessions. Remind them, if necessary, that Jeremiah is one of God's friends and messengers. In this Bible story, God has given Jeremiah a message to give to the people. Jeremiah is saying what God has said; and Baruch is busy writing all the words down.

3 When the children have completed their story pictures, suggest they turn the paper over and fill the other side with 'writing' (real words or squiggly patterns are fine).

4 Show them how to roll up the paper from both ends to make a scroll.

For older children

Listening to God

 minutes

Why: to encourage young people to listen to God
With: sticky notes, pens, background music, Bibles

1 Hand out sticky notes and pens. As you play some quiet background music, encourage the young people to close their eyes and, in the quietness, try to listen to what God might be saying to them. Explain that God speaks to people in many different ways, and not necessarily in the same way to every person! God can speak through his words in the Bible, through our thoughts, emotions, the words of others, through everyday objects, the beauty around us, the quiet and the loud! Give an example of how God has spoken to you to start them thinking.

2 Encourage the young people to write down anything they think God might have been saying to them on to their sticky notes. Have extra available in case.

3 If appropriate, give space for the young people to share what they have written. Encourage the young people to keep their sticky notes in their Bibles, or somewhere safe, as a reminder. If the young people feel God has said something to them for someone else, exercise a little caution and judge whether it would be good to share that with the other person. Be sensitive to any young people who may feel that God did not say anything to them. Reassure them of his love and encourage them to keep listening in many different ways – God speaks to everyone, but sometimes it takes time for us to recognise it and to hear what he is saying!

4 Close with a prayer asking Jesus to continue to speak to us and to help us create the time and space to have listening ears.

THE LEARN AND REMEMBER VERSE

'Even before I speak, you already know what I will say.'

Psalm 139:4

Say the verse to the children, pausing before the words 'speak' and 'say', and letting them say those words. Ask the children how God can know what we are going to say. Explain that he knows what is in our minds!

Find a poster for this Learn and remember verse on page 35.

You could also use the song 'Even before I speak', on the *Bitesize Bible Songs 2* CD, available from Scripture Union.

Use with **Bible story picture**
Jeremiah's scroll Jeremiah 36

SESSION 4

Down a well

Bible:
Jeremiah 38:1–13

Aim: To speak out for God whatever the consequences

CORE PROGRAMME

For 3 to 14s

Bible story with drama

⑩ - ⑮ *minutes*

Why: to speak out for God whatever the consequences
With: chairs or screens, headdress to represent Jeremiah (optional), SU *Bible Timeline* or the *Big Bible Storybook Timeline* (optional, see page 96 for details)

1 Down the well

Arrange chairs or screens (or other furniture available in your room) in a circle to make a well. Sit on the floor inside your 'well' with the children and put on the headdress. Tell the children that every time you say 'well', they should say 'Poor Jeremiah! Keep going!'

2 Tell the story

Story: Hello! I'm Jeremiah and I'm so pleased you've come to keep me company at the bottom of this horrible well. The sides are so steep I can't get out, and it's cold and dark! I'm glad the water has dried up – although it's still a bit muddy! You're probably wondering why I'm down here.

Well, let me tell you. I've been telling God's message to the kings and the people, but they refuse to pay any attention. One of the kings even burned God's message. I felt like giving up, I can tell you. But God never gives up, so even when things are hard I have to keep going.

Well, the last message God gave me was not good! God said it was time to give in to our enemies and let them take over Jerusalem. If we didn't, the Babylonians would capture the city anyway and we would all die. He said that if we surrendered, at least we would stay alive. Four of the king's officials were furious when they heard me speak and rushed off to King Zedekiah. 'You should put Jeremiah to death, because he is making the soldiers and everyone else lose hope. He isn't trying to help our people; he's trying to harm them.'

The king agreed! He told his officials to do what they wanted with me. It's as well for me that they didn't kill me on the spot! Instead they dragged me off and let me down with ropes into this well. They probably hope I'll starve to death!

3 Climb out

Take off the Jeremiah headdress and ask the children how Jeremiah must have felt. Was he right to do what God said even when it made life so difficult for him? Ask what they think will happen next.

Explain that to find out they need to climb out of the well and go to the courtyard of the palace guards. Rearrange the chairs or screens into a square and sit down again. Put on your headdress and go back into character as Jeremiah.

4 Tell the story part 2

Story: Hello again! Well, you can see that I've escaped. But I didn't climb out – that well was far too deep. The most amazing thing happened! One of God's followers, Ebedmelech, heard what had happened and he went to see the king. 'Your majesty,' he said, 'Jeremiah is a prophet, and those men were wrong to throw him into a well. He'll starve down there.'

'Take 30 of my soldiers and pull Jeremiah out before he dies,' said the king.

Ebedmelech gathered up some rags and lowered them down to me. I put the rags under my arms and then the rope and the men pulled me out. And here I am! I'm still a prisoner but at least I'm not down the well. Isn't God good? I obey him and he looks after me really well!

5 Think

Ask the children if they can think of other people in the Bible who kept going when it was difficult. If you have a *Bible Timeline* you could use it here. Thank God that he will always help us, even when things are difficult.

Praise

 minutes

Why: to see consequences of speaking for God

1 Invite each child to fold a sheet of paper into a wide concertina and draw a person shape on the front fold. When they cut round the person, remind them to leave the ends of the hands uncut at the fold so that they unfold a row of paper people.

2 Encourage them to write their name on the end person, then to write the names of anyone who has helped them learn about God on the other people.

3 Invite them to hold the 'people' up and thank God for these people who have spoken out for him and helped them.

Cartoons

 minutes

Why: to think about the consequences of speaking up for God

With: copies of page 33 for each child

1 Give out copies of the incomplete cartoon strips from page 33. (If possible, enlarge them for younger children.)

2 Read the cartoons together and talk about what might happen next – what might be the consequence for the person who has been speaking up for God?

3 Challenge the children to complete the cartoons individually. Encourage them to do one cartoon with a positive consequence, and one with a negative one. Display the different completed cartoons around the room.

Tableaux

 minutes

Why: to think about where we might speak out for God

1 Encourage the children to work in pairs to make their bodies into a frozen image that shows how a person could speak out for God in a given situation. (Allow some thinking time before they have to freeze.) Suggested situations: talking to parents; at school; at church; with a school bully; with a Christian friend; with a good (but not believing) friend.

2 Chat together about whether it is easy, or hard, to speak up for God. Encourage the children to pray for one another.

EXTENSION IDEAS

Activities for younger children

Game

 minutes

Why: to think about speaking out
With: a blindfold, a soft toy

1 Sit in a circle with one child outside the circle and blindfolded or with eyes tightly shut. Encourage the children to pass the toy around the circle until the blindfolded child shouts, 'Stop!' Invite the child holding the toy to stand up and sing or say something. (Keep this fun and light-hearted.) If the blindfolded child guesses the identity of the singer, they exchange places. Any child who finds this difficult should just pass the toy on.

2 Talk about how the children felt. Say that today they will hear about someone who spoke out for God when it was very difficult.

Bible story picture

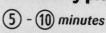 *minutes*

Why: to discover that God looks after his people
With: a copy of the picture from page 34 (printed on A4 paper) for each child or enlarged copies for group use, art and craft materials

1 You can use the picture as an introduction to the Bible story or to help you review the story together.

2 Give out the Bible story pictures and sound relieved as you do so: Jeremiah was down a well but – good – now some kind men are pulling him to safety.

3 Make sure that the children know what a 'well' is; then ask: 'Did Jeremiah fall down the well?' (*No!*) 'Did Jeremiah want to be down the well?' (*No!*) 'Did someone put him down the well?' (*Yes!*) But who would do that? Find out in the Bible story.

For older children

Chat

(5) *minutes*

Why: to see that speaking up can be hard

1 Ask the children if they've ever found speaking up for God difficult. Chat about the different things people can do to make it difficult for us (laugh at us, tell us we're stupid, ignore us, spread gossip about us). As the children say their ideas, write them on separate sticky notes.

2 When you have six or more ideas, challenge the children to organise them in order, according to how difficult they find (or imagine) them to cope with.

3 Say that today they will see how Jeremiah spoke for God even in a tough situation.

THE LEARN AND REMEMBER VERSE

'Even before I speak, you already know what I will say.'

Psalm 139:4

Get each child to ask the rest of the group obscure questions about themselves, to see how well they know each other. God knows everything about us – even what we will say next!

Repeat the verse several times, starting in a whisper and building up to a crescendo.

Find a poster for this Learn and remember verse on page 35.

You could also use the song 'Even before I speak', on the *Bitesize Bible Songs 2* CD, available from Scripture Union.

Incomplete cartoon strips for use with **Cartoons**

Use with **Bible story picture**
Jeremiah in the well Jeremiah 38:1–13

Psalm 139:4

'Even before I speak, you already know what I will say.'

SERIES INTRODUCTION

HOW SHOULD WE PRAY?

Explore the answer to this question and discover that God speaks and listens to us.

BIBLE BACKGROUND FOR YOU

We all know that prayer should be a natural part of the Christian life, but if we are honest, we all struggle at times. The next four sessions give us an opportunity to be encouraged and challenged afresh by what Jesus says about prayer.

The Lord's Prayer is a model for our own praying, demonstrating a concern for God's honour and reputation, for his values to be displayed in the world, for our relationships with others as well as for our own needs. The remaining sessions reinforce the message that prayer is about relationship, trust, dependence, humility and perseverance.

Those in our groups will learn a lot from how we pray as well as from what we say about prayer. But they will not have the same difficulties that we have – prayer can often be more natural for children than for adults. Do our prayers show a simple trust in God? In what ways do they demonstrate a concern for his honour and for his rule? To what extent can we lay aside our sense of self-importance so that we can receive God's blessing? And how far are we prepared to learn from children about the simple, trusting relationship with God that is the basis of prayer?

For your small group with a wide age range

It is encouraging for our children to know that we can talk to God about any aspect of our lives at any time, and more importantly to know that God wants to listen! This series is an opportunity to pray together in different ways which are engaging and fun, not just a duty. Let older children try more adventurous ideas in the Extension activities while younger ones enjoy those which are more suitable to their abilities. Do try to demonstrate that prayer is something to be enjoyed together as well as individually. With a small group, everyone gets a chance to take part!

Resources for ministry

Ultimate Creative Prayer is crammed full of creative and imaginative ways to get praying. Ideas include prayers to draw and make, prayers to shout and sing, prayers to pray alone and pray together. Inside you'll find all the instructions and guidance you need to help your group pray and grow together.

Highlights from *LightLive*

Go to the 'Search *LightLive*' tab at www.lightlive.org and enter this session's Bible reference to find:

- 'Audio Bible story': a regular mp3 download for 3–7s
- 'Learn and remember': a PowerPoint of a Bible verse to learn, for 5–11s (see also page 59)
- 'Presentation': an activity with animation for 11–14s

ULTIMATE
Creative prayer

SESSION 1

Pray like Jesus

Bible:
Luke 11:1–4;
Matthew 6:5–15

Aim: To pray knowing, from Jesus' example and teaching, that God wants us to talk to him

CORE PROGRAMME

For 3 to 14s

Bible story with drawing

 ⑮ - ⑳ *minutes*

Why: to see from Jesus' example and teaching that God wants us to talk to him

With: SU *Bible Timeline* or the *Big Bible Storybook Timeline* (optional, see page 96 for details), copy of zigzag book template on page 38 for each child, glitter (optional)

1 Make

Tell the children that if we copy Jesus we will always get things right. For example, if we look at how he talked to God, we will know how to talk or pray to God, too. Today they are going to learn the prayer Jesus taught his friends. We call it the Lord's Prayer. Give each child a copy of page 38 and help them to make their zigzag books.

2 Listen

Explain that together you are going to look at each part of Jesus' prayer, but first you are going to read it from the Bible. Read Matthew 6:9–13. Encourage the children to follow it in the zigzag book.

3 Talk, draw and pray

First panel: Say that Jesus called God Father. Ask what a good father is like. (Be aware of children who may not have a good relationship with their father.) Say that when Jesus prayed he used the Aramaic word for 'Daddy', which tells us that we can talk to God in the same way we talk to a kind dad. Ask them to think about what they would like to say to him as they colour in the word 'Father'.

Second panel: Jesus says that God's name is holy. God is awesome and perfect and his name is precious. Ask the children to write the word 'holy' several times in the panel using their favourite colours. As they do so, encourage them to tell God how precious he is to them.

Third panel: Jesus asks that God's kingdom will be established on the earth. We too can pray that people will decide to live God's way. Suggest the children pray for the world as they colour in the globe.

Fourth panel: Jesus says we should ask for the food we need. We can ask God for other things we need, too, and thank him for what he gives us. Discuss together some of these

things, then suggest the children talk to God as they draw their favourite food.

Fifth panel: Jesus says we should ask God to forgive us for the things we have done wrong. Because of Jesus' death on the cross we know that God will forgive us when we say sorry. And we must also remember to forgive other people when they have hurt us. Encourage the children to talk to God as they draw a cross on the panel and write 'forgive us'.

Sixth panel: Jesus knew what it was like to be tempted to do wrong. We know we need God's help to do and say what is right. Allow time for the children to talk to God about this part of the prayer as they look at the picture and write 'no' beside the wrong thing to do and 'yes' beside the right thing.

4 Chat

Look at the SU *Bible Timeline*. Say that Jesus gave us the Lord's Prayer when he was teaching, but he was also busy doing other things. Ask the children to think of some of these, such as travelling, preaching, healing. But even though Jesus was very busy, he still found time for one very important thing. Read Mark 1:35. Jesus got up early so that he could be alone with God to pray. Sometimes he spent a very long time in prayer. Read Luke 6:12.

37

Zigzag book template for use with **Bible story with drawing**

Glue or tape here.

Give us our food for today.

Fold

Forgive us for doing wrong, as we forgive others.

Fold

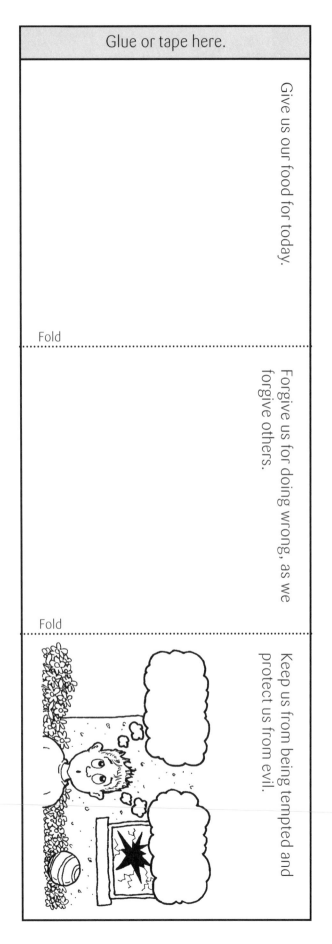

Keep us from being tempted and protect us from evil.

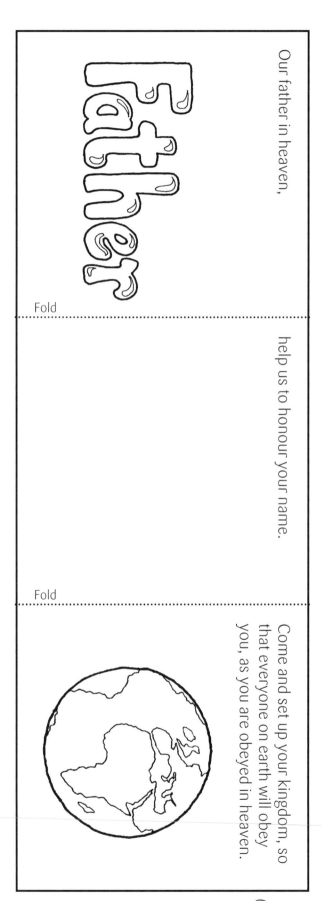

Our father in heaven,

Fold

help us to honour your name.

Fold

Come and set up your kingdom, so that everyone on earth will obey you, as you are obeyed in heaven.

CORE PROGRAMME CONTINUED

5 Think

Explain that even though we can pray anywhere and at any time, it's good to copy Jesus and have a special time when we talk to God.

Movement and prayer

 - ⑮ *minutes*

Why: to see how we can use the pattern of the Lord's Prayer in our own prayers
With: a dice (or numbers 1 to 6 in a container)

1 Tell the children that they are going to use the pattern of Jesus' prayer to help them pray. Number and label individual sheets of paper: 1 Father; 2 Holy; 3 The earth; 4 Please; 5 Sorry; 6 Help us. Write on each sheet of paper some ideas to pray about this week. For example: for 'Father', we can trust God our Father during difficult times. Place the sheets of paper around the room.

2 Standing in the centre of the room, ask a child to throw the dice (or pull out a number). Invite the children to move to the sheet of paper with that number. Say a brief prayer, using the first idea on the list.

3 Return to the centre and repeat step 2 until everyone has had a turn.

Praying together

⑤ *minutes*

Why: to encourage the children to pray together

1 Invite everyone to sit in a circle. Ask the children to pray silently for the people sitting on either side of them. Explain that even if they don't know much about these people, God knows all about them and what is best for them.

2 Go around the circle in turn, asking each child who they would like everyone to pray for. Don't pressurise them to contribute if they prefer not to. If you know of particular family circumstances, you might like to sensitively suggest that everyone could pray for them.

3 Pray for the things mentioned and allow time for any of the children to pray aloud if they want to. Pray on the children's behalf, if necessary.

Prayer scrapbook

⑩ *minutes*

Why: to talk to God using pictures and artwork
With: a scrapbook, magazine pictures, photographs, children's artwork, a marker pen

1 Enjoy working together to make a scrapbook (or poster or collage) of pictures that the children want to talk to God about. Let them choose what to include and do as much of the cutting and sticking as they can.

2 Add words of thanks or comments, written on paper, recording the children's formal or casual prayers. Give the book a title that shows it has been made by everyone and is a group production.

3 When the book is finished, turn the pages one at a time and encourage the children to talk about what is shown and to use the written words (and other words of their own) to talk to God.

4 Keep the book where the children can look through it again, on their own or with others. (If the children enjoyed this activity, repeat it in other sessions with different themes.)

EXTENSION IDEAS

Activities for younger children

Miming game

 **⑩ - ⑮** *minutes*

Why: to remember that we can follow Jesus' example and pray at busy times

With: a timer with a loud ring, a large sheet of paper (optional)

1 Remind the children of Jesus' busy life. Say that today we may not walk around villages, healing and teaching as he did, but we have busy lives too. Ask the children to name all the things they have to do and, if you wish, write them on a large sheet of paper. You could put them under different headings, such as home, school, clubs and play, or you could use different colours.

2 Tell the children you are going to set the timer and suggest a place where they are pretending to be. Encourage them to mime things they do at that place until the timer rings, then to shout out, 'Don't forget to pray!'

3 Play several times, mentioning different places and varying the length of time on the timer.

Bible story picture

 **⑤ - ⑩** *minutes*

Why: to talk and listen to God

With: a copy of the picture on page 41 (printed on A4 paper) for each child or enlarged copies for group use, art and craft materials, an adult helper, rugs, cushions, books of prayers, pictures, items for the children to hold such as a small wooden cross, a piece of soft fabric, a favourite cuddly toy

1 You can use the picture as an introduction to the Bible story or to help you review the story together.

2 During each session this series, set out an area of your meeting space as a 'prayer corner'. Make the area comfortable, with cushions and rugs to sit on. Provide things to look at, admire and handle. Include pictures from the Bible story and art materials to decorate them.

3 Arrange to have a leader available to join any children in the prayer corner, to listen and encourage their exploration and to suggest ways to pray, as appropriate. Keep this low-key, welcoming, unpressured and optional.

For older children

Discussion

⑤ - ⑩ *minutes*

Why: to understand that prayer is communication with God

1 As a group, list all the different ways we communicate with each other. Try to think of every conceivable way – from talking to text messaging, from online social networking to sign language and telephone calls.

2 Say that God wants us to communicate with him. Ask the children how they might do that.

3 Practise communicating with God in some of the ways the children and young people have identified.

4 Say that they don't need to use mobile phones or write emails because they have a 'direct line' to God, which is never busy!

THE LEARN AND REMEMBER VERSE

'Don't worry about anything, but in all your prayers ask God for what you need, always asking him with a thankful heart.'

Philippians 4:6

Encourage the children to use actions to accompany the phrases 'Don't worry', 'prayers', 'ask God', 'what you need' and 'thankful heart'.

Find a poster for this Learn and remember verse on page 59.

You could also use the song 'Don't worry', on the *Bitesize Bible Songs 2* CD, available from Scripture Union.

Use with **Bible story picture**
Jesus talks with God Luke 11:1–4; Matthew 6:5–15

SESSION 2
Ask, search and knock

Bible:
Luke 11:5–13

Aim: To be inspired to talk with God in the way he wants us to

CORE PROGRAMME

For 3 to 14s

Radio show

 20 minutes

Why: to be inspired to talk with God in the way he wants us to

With: recording equipment (optional), percussion instruments as listed below, pictures and text for 'Radio show' from page 43 (optional), SU *Bible Timeline* or *Big Bible Storybook Timeline* (see page 96 for details)

1 *Bible Timeline*

Challenge the children to find the picture of Jesus sitting talking to people on the *Timeline*. Tell them that they are going to make a radio show about the time when Jesus talked to his disciples about prayer. Explain that they will add the sound effects.

2 Rehearse

Say that the first part of the show is a story about a man who needed help from his friend. Invite the children to sit in a circle. Give out the instruments in the order below. If you have fewer than 11 children, give

some more than one instrument. You could use the available pictures and words to help each child remember the sound effect they are making.

Child 1: a cymbal
Child 2: shakers
Child 3: a drum
Child 4: a whistle
Child 5: makes yawning sound
Child 6: sandpaper blocks
Child 7: wood block
Child 8: bunch of keys
Child 9: wood block hit three times
Child 10: saying, 'I need three loaves of bread. My friend has come to visit and I have no food for him.'
Child 11: saying, 'Don't bother me now. We're all asleep.'

Encourage each child, in order, to practise making their sound effect: using their instruments, making their noise or saying their words.

3 Record

Explain that as you tell the story, the children must do their sound effect when you point to them. If possible, record the drama to play back later.

Story: There was once a man who needed help from his friend in the middle of the night *(cue child 1)*. He set off along the sandy road to his friend's house *(cue child 2)*. When he arrived, the house was in darkness so he banged on the door *(cue child 3)*. But there was no answer. All he could hear was the sound of snoring from an upstairs room *(child 4)*.

The man really needed his friend's help, so he knocked again, and again *(child 3)*. Eventually he heard a huge yawn *(child 4 and child 5)*. The man looked up to see his friend opening the window *(child 6)*. The man squinted up at his friend *(cue child 10)*. His friend yawned, spoke and then closed the window *(child 5, child 11 and child 6)*.

But the man kept on asking *(child 10)* and asking *(child 10)* and asking *(child 10)*. At last he heard footsteps *(child 7)*. Then the door opened *(child 8)*. He reached out into the dark and placed three loaves of bread into the man's hands *(child 9)*.

4 Pause

Stop recording and challenge the children to think about the story. How did the man talk with his friend? How did his friend respond? How can we talk with God? How does God respond when we talk with him?

5 Research

Say that in the second part of our radio show we will find out how Jesus used this story to teach us about how we can talk with God. Read Luke 11:9–13. Explain that God is our heavenly Father. God wants us to be brave and confident when we talk with him, like the man in the story who asked for bread. He wants us to talk with him and trust that he hears and gives us good things.

Pictures and text for use with **Radio show**

I need three loaves of bread.

My friend has come to visit and I have no food for him.

Don't bother me now.

We're all asleep.

CORE PROGRAMME CONTINUED

6 Cast interviews

Give the children a few minutes to think of a response to the question, 'How does God want us to talk with him?' Record their responses.

7 On air

Listen to the radio show. Share the recording with other groups or with the congregation.

Prayer walk

Up to *minutes*

Why: to pray in different places and in different ways
With: adult supervision

1 Arrange a suitable route to different parts of the building or outside if this can be done safely. Make this an 'event': you are going to be doing something exciting!

2 Say these words from Psalm 116: 'I love the Lord, because he hears me; he listens to my prayers. He listens to me every time I call to him.'

3 Walk along your route together. While you walk, sing or 'lah' a worship song that you all know well. Pause from time to time and talk to God. Use different modes of praying each time you stop: spoken words, singing, shouting, quietness or praying silently, mime. You could also try different stances: standing, sitting, kneeling, lying down.

4 As you return, remind the children of the words you said from the Bible: God has heard your prayers and he always listens when we talk with him. How does that make them feel?

Stepping stones prayers

 minutes

Why: to keep talking to God in the way that he wants
With: one large paper circle, at least 30 smaller circles

1 Place the large circle on the floor in the middle of the room. Divide the smaller circles into three sets.

On set 1, invite children to write a word or phrase that describes God.

On set 2, ask them to write something they would like to ask God for themselves.

On set 3, write something they want to ask God for someone else

2 Spread the smaller circles in three different areas of the floor. Starting from the large circle, invite children to use them like stepping stones to 'step' across the set 1 circles, calling out the word as they stand on that circle. Repeat with the prayers for yourselves (set 2), and then with those for other people (set 3).

Talking with God

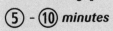 *minutes*

Why: to talk with God about our needs
With: speech bubbles for 'Talking with God' from page 45

1 Ask the children what we can learn from Jesus' story. Remind them that God wants us to keep talking with him and that he listens to us when we talk to him.

2 Encourage the children to think about something they would like to ask God for. Divert them away from 'a new bike' type prayers, towards help for themselves or someone they know. Encourage the children to write or draw their prayers on the speech bubbles.

3 Invite the children to take it in turns to place their speech bubble into a central pile, saying their prayer out loud as they do so.

4 Give them more speech bubbles to take home. Challenge them to write more prayers and carry on talking to God this week.

EXTENSION IDEAS
Activities for younger children

Active discussion

 minutes

Why: to think about how we ask God for the things we need
With: some fruit cut into small portions, a small item to hide

1 Be aware of food hygiene and allergy issues. Explain that the fruit is for sharing. Encourage everyone to say, 'Please...' as you pass it around. Say that praying can sometimes be like asking. We ask God for what we need.

2 Play 'Hunt the thimble' using the small item you have chosen. Hide it, then let the group look for it, repeating the game several times. Say that talking to God can be like searching for something. We keep on talking to him, just like they kept on looking until they found the item.

3 Play a game with two or three children, with an adult knocking at a door, acting out today's Bible story. Give everyone a chance to play. Then say that praying can be like knocking. We keep asking for what we need, just as they kept knocking until the door was opened. Jesus told his friends to 'ask, search and knock' when they asked God for what they needed.

Bible story picture

5 - 10 *minutes*

Why: to hear that God wants us to talk with him and that he listens to us
With: a copy of the picture on page 46 (printed on A4 paper) for each child or enlarged copies for group use, art and craft materials, an adult helper, rugs, cushions, books of prayers, pictures, items for the children to hold such as a small wooden cross, a piece of soft fabric, a favourite cuddly toy

1 You can use the picture as an introduction to the Bible story or to help you review the story together.

2 During each session of this *Mosaic* series about 'Talking with God', set out an area of your meeting space as a 'prayer corner'. Make the area comfortable, with cushions and rugs to sit on. Provide things to look at, admire and handle. Include pictures from the Bible story and art materials to decorate them.

3 Arrange to have a leader available to join any children in the prayer corner, to listen and encourage their exploration and to suggest ways to pray, as appropriate. Keep this low-key, welcoming, unpressured and optional.

For older children

Visual prayer

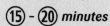 **minutes**

Why: to pray in the ways the passage has suggested

1 Make sure everyone has a sheet of paper and invite them to draw a large Venn diagram with three intersecting circles so that they all intersect at the centre.

2 In each of the circles the young people should write one of the following: 'Ask', 'Seek', 'Knock'.

3 Ask the group to list in the 'Ask' circle things that they want to ask God for – their needs. In the 'Seek' circle, they should write where they want to be – what they want God to help them with as they journey through life. In the 'Knock' circle they should list anything that is blocking their path, and things they would like to overcome. Explain that no one will need to see what they have written; this is between them and God.

4 In the central area of intersection they should draw an image that represents God to them, and in the three overlapping areas they should write the three words: 'Trust in God'.

5 Remind the young people that God wants us to ask for what we need, and to trust him to provide for us.

THE LEARN AND REMEMBER VERSE

'Don't worry about anything, but in all your prayers ask God for what you need, always asking him with a thankful heart.'

Philippians 4:6

Write each word on a card. Place all the 'short words' (one to three letters) and all the 'long words' (four letters +) together face down. Challenge the children to choose five short and three long words and try to put them in order, then use them as prompts to say the whole verse.

Find a poster for this Learn and remember verse on page 59.

You could also use the song 'Don't worry', on the *Bitesize Bible Songs 2* CD, available from Scripture Union.

PHOTOCOPIABLE PART
Speech bubbles for use with **Talking with God**

Use with **Bible story picture**
God wants us to talk to him Luke 11:5–13

SESSION 3

Never give up

Bible:
Luke 18:1–8

Aim: To pray, understanding that God is listening and wants us to keep talking to him

CORE PROGRAMME

For 3 to 14s

Prayer activities

⑮ - ⑳ *minutes*

Why: to pray, understanding that God is listening and wants us to keep talking to him
With: an orange, a table knife (not sharp)

1 Explanation

As you talk to the children, peel the orange. Explain that sometimes Jesus taught people about God using a type of story called a parable. A parable works on two layers. The top layer is like the skin of an orange; it tells the basic story. But, once you peel away the top layer, you might find something else – a message about how we should live God's way. Show the children the peeled orange, and offer everyone a piece. (Peel more oranges if you have a large group of children.) Say that we can read the parables today, and learn more about God. This is like food for our minds. Challenge the children to remember some stories that Jesus told, and then to point on the *Bible Timeline* to when he told them.

2 Read the Bible verses

Choose a confident reader to read Luke 18:1–8 from a child-friendly Bible.

3 Act out the story

Invite the children to get into pairs. If there is an uneven number of children, either get one pair to work with the narrator, or join one child with a leader. Explain that they are going to act out the story, either as it is portrayed in the Bible text or as a modern-day equivalent. Encourage the children to refer to the Bible verses and use them as the basis for their script. Allow time for everyone to work on this. Make sure you (or one of the other leaders) visit each group to encourage them and help them if necessary. Give each pair a chance to show everyone what they have done, but if your group is too large to do that, one pair could join with another pair and take it in turns to show each other.

4 Game

Explain that everyone is going to play a game to find out the answer to the question 'How can we keep praying?' Ask the children to form two equal-sized teams and line up at one end of the room.

Challenge each child to run/hop/jump (whatever is appropriate) to the other end of the room, get back again and tag the next team member. The first team to finish this wins. Explain that they are going to do this relay twice. The first time, they can't shout any words of encouragement or make any noise to cheer on their teammates. The second time, they can go crazy and shout and cheer for all they are worth! When they have finished, ask them which was more fun and which encouraged them to go faster.

5 Discussion

Now ask them if they can work out the answer to the question: 'How can we keep praying?' Say that it's much easier to run with a crowd cheering you on, and that it's also easier to pray when you have people encouraging you. You can help each other to pray by: praying together in this group, asking each other if they have been praying, sharing the answers they've had to prayers and asking people to pray for them. All of these encourage us to keep on praying. Ask the children to suggest other ways to encourage each other.

CORE PROGRAMME CONTINUED

Prayer walk

(15) – (30) *minutes*

Why: to talk to God about anything
With: sheet for 'Prayer walk' (page 49) (optional)

1 Prepare your walking route beforehand, keeping the children's ages in mind. Remember to ask for parental permission if you are going outside. Decide whether to pray during the walk or when you get back. Use the prayer sheet (page 49) if you wish.

2 Tell the children that, as you walk, you are going to find things to talk to God about. For example, thanking him for flowers, places to play, our homes; or asking him for things. In the story, the widow wanted the judge to put things right for her, so you might talk to God about things that aren't right, for example, a place that has been spoiled, or people without homes.

3 Remind the children that they can talk to God wherever they walk.

Prayer box

(10) *minutes*

Why: to talk with God
With: a large cardboard box with an opening lid and ready-cut posting slot, gift wrap, objects that prompt the children to pray

1 Ask the children to help you decorate the box, wrapping it with paper. While you work together, explain that you are making a prayer box. It will be a place to put ideas of things that the children want to tell God about.

2 Let the children draw their prayer ideas on paper, fold them up and post them in the box. (You can add other prayer-pointers like toys, shells, pebbles, photos, books of prayers, anything that works as a prompt.)

3 Sit in a circle, shake the box and open the lid. Let each child in turn take out a paper. What does it show? Encourage the child to talk to God about it now. (If they are shy, say some prayer words that they can echo.)

4 The prayer box could become a regular feature of your group, with children adding their prayer ideas in each session.

Crafty prayer

(5) – (10) *minutes*

Why: to help the children pray creatively
With: copies of page 50 (there are two templates per page; each child will need a template), scissors, paper clips

1 Give each child a copy of the prayer whizzer from page 50 and encourage them to cut out the shape and cut down the middle line.

2 On the two rectangular strips invite them to write two things they would like to pray about every day for a week.

3 Help the children to fold the two strips at the fold line where indicated – one forward and the other backwards. Show them how to push a paper clip onto the pointed end of the single arm. If they stand on a chair and throw their prayer whizzer into the air, it will glide to the floor, spinning like a helicopter rotor. Do this twice, and as it falls each time, encourage them to pray for one of their prayer items.

4 Encourage them to do this every day in the coming week!

Sheet for use with **Prayer walk**

prayer walk

Talk to God as you walk along. See if you can see any of these things.
You might like to tick the box or draw a picture.

something beautiful. Say **thank you**. ☐	something to say '**please**' for. ☐
A place where people are helped. **Pray** for the people there. ☐	something to say '**sorry**' for. ☐
A happy place. Say **thank you**. ☐	A creature God has made. **Praise** God! ☐

Template for use with **Crafty prayer**

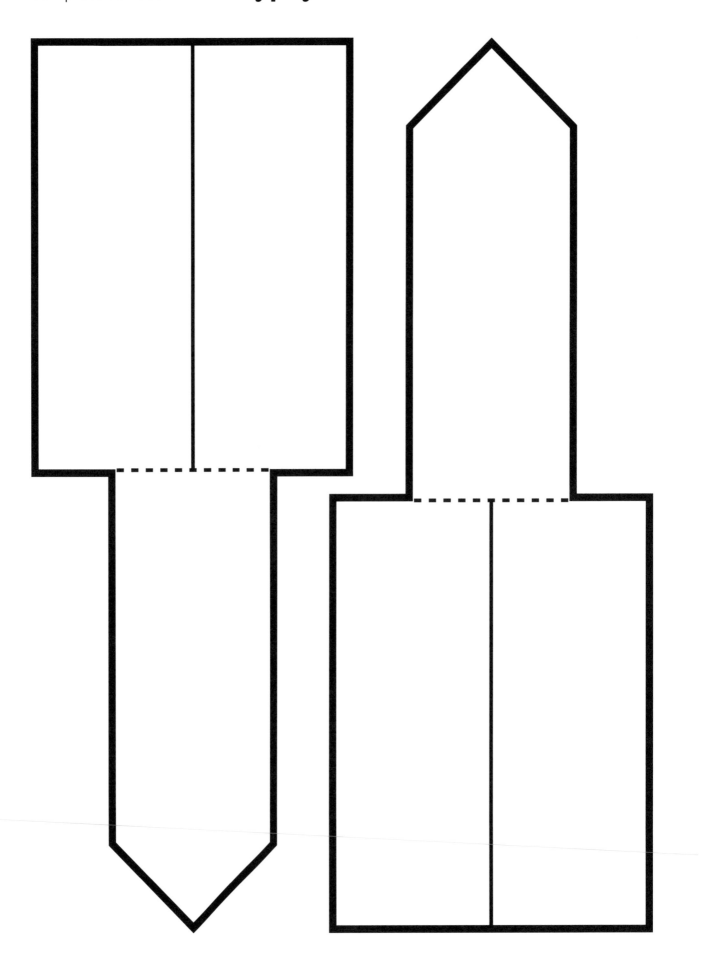

EXTENSION IDEAS

Activities for younger children

Prayer reminder

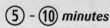 **minutes**

Why: to encourage each other, remembering that God will always listen to our prayers

1 Teach the children the following acronym: PINGU (Prayer Instruction: Never Give Up). Write it on a sheet of paper so that they can see how the first letters spell PINGU. Say that this is a good way to remember what Jesus taught us about God. We should never give up talking to God because he never gives up listening to us. Practise the acronym together so that the children know what each letter means. If they wish, they can write it down.

2 Sit in a circle. Encourage the children to take turns to whisper 'PINGU' to the next person.

3 Stand up, join hands and say together: 'Thank you, God, for always listening.'

Bible story picture

 minutes

Why: to discover we can always talk with God
With: a copy of the picture on page 52 (printed on A4 paper) for each child or enlarged copies for group use, art and craft materials, an adult helper, rugs, cushions, books of prayers, pictures, items for the children to hold such as a small wooden cross, a piece of soft fabric, a favourite cuddly toy

1 You can use the picture as an introduction to the Bible story or to help you review the story together.

2 During each session in this Mosaic series about 'Talking with God', set out an area of your meeting space as a 'prayer corner'. Make the area comfortable, with cushions and rugs to sit on. Provide things to look at, admire and handle. Include pictures from the Bible story and art materials to decorate them.

3 Arrange to have a leader available to join any children in the prayer corner, to listen and encourage their exploration and to suggest ways to pray, as appropriate. Keep this low-key, welcoming, unpressured and optional.

For older children

Prayer diary

10 minutes

Why: to respond to the teaching with persistent prayer
With: a notebook

1 Before the session, buy a nice, hardback, lined exercise book or notebook.

2 Tell the group that this is going to be a 'Group prayer journal'. Explain that it will be a way of keeping a record of prayers and how they have been responded to. They should feel able to write in it the things they have been praying for.

3 Pass the book around as you share prayer requests and write them down under today's date. Invite the young people to pray for the situations listed.

4 When you pray in your next session, bring out the book and ask if any of those prayers have been answered. If the young people don't feel that they have, encourage them to keep praying persistently. Thank God for any answered prayers and make a note of the answers in the prayer journal.

5 If you manage to keep the journal going for a long time, it's good to look back to see what concerns have been prayed about and what God has done. Sometimes it is hard to see God at work day by day, but it is encouraging to look back over a longer period of time.

THE LEARN AND REMEMBER VERSE

'Don't worry about anything, / but in all your prayers ask God for what you need, / always asking him with a thankful heart.'

Philippians 4:6

Notice how the verse has been divided into three sections above. Divide the children into three groups and ask them to say a section each. When they have said the verse like that several times, they should see if they can remember the whole verse.

Find a poster for this Learn and remember verse on page 59.

You could also use the song 'Don't worry', on the *Bitesize Bible Songs 2* CD, available from Scripture Union.

Use with **Bible story picture**
God will always hear us Luke 18:1–8

SESSION 4

Smug or sorry

Bible:
Luke 18:9–14

Aim: To pray, knowing that God wants us to be honest with him

CORE PROGRAMME

For 3 to 14s

Bible story with visual aids

⑩ – ⑮ minutes

Why: to know that God wants us to be honest with him when we pray

With: a fringed shawl, a cloak, two small boxes, two lengths of ribbon, safety pins, labels; SU *Bible Timeline* or *Big Bible Storybook Timeline* (optional, see page 96 for details)

1 Prepare

In advance, pin a label saying 'You are forgiven' to the inside of the cloak. Try to ensure that the children don't see this until you reveal it later.

2 Dress up

Invite the children to find the SU *Bible Timeline* picture of Jesus teaching. Challenge them to remember the stories that you looked at in previous sessions. Say that today they're going to hear a story Jesus told about two people who thought they were very good and looked down on others. Choose two volunteers and dress one in the shawl and one in the cloak.

Read Luke 18:10 from a child-friendly Bible. Look at the man in the shawl first. Say that this is the Pharisee. He is wearing a prayer shawl. Say that he would put this on every time he went to the Temple to pray. Use the ribbon to tie one of the boxes gently to the Pharisee's forehead and the other around his arm. Tell the children that these boxes contain Bible verses to remind the person wearing them that they must keep all of God's laws. Because of the prayer shawl and the little boxes, everyone can see that this man's clothes are saying, 'Look at me! I am a very good person.' Pin a label saying, 'I am good' on his shawl.

Look at the man in the cloak. Explain that this man is the tax collector. Everyone has to pay tax to the Romans, who are ruling over them, and this man collects the money. Perhaps he collects more money than he should and keeps the extra so that he can afford expensive things. This man's clothes say, 'Look at me! I have lots of money – and some of it has been stolen from you!' Pin a label on the tax collector's cloak saying, 'I am not a good person'.

3 Listen and think

Ask the children if they can remember why the two men went into the Temple (*to pray*). Say that they are going to listen to those prayers.

Read verses 11 and 12 of Luke 18. What did the man say he was like? What did he say he wasn't like? Does he still sound good?

Pin another label on the Pharisee's shawl saying, 'I am very good'.

Read verse 13. Ask: Why wouldn't the tax collector look up? What does 'pounded his chest' (CEV) mean? Why did he say he was such a sinner? Does the tax collector still sound bad? Pin another label on his cloak saying, 'I am a very bad person'.

Say that here are two men talking to God: one very good and one very bad. Encourage the children to tell you what they think God will think of all this. Take the shawl off the Pharisee. The 'I am good' labels have come off too. His goodness and his prayers are only on the outside.

Take the cloak off the tax collector. 'Discover' the label inside. Read it out: 'You are forgiven'. Point out that the 'I am bad' labels have been removed and the tax collector has been forgiven, right through to his inside. God knew that the tax collector really meant his prayer and was asking God to forgive him for being bad. God heard his prayer and forgave him. Read verse 14a.

CORE PROGRAMME CONTINUED

4 **Pray**

Ask the two volunteers to sit down and spread out the shawl and cloak where everyone can see them. Say that they remind us that God wants us to talk to him honestly when we pray, not pretending in any way. That's great because God knows and loves us so well.

Have a time of quiet when the children can say whatever they want to God. Finish by saying together: 'Thank you, God, for knowing and loving us.'

Prayer heart

 minutes

Why: to pray, knowing that God wants us to be honest with him
With: picture for 'Prayer heart' (page 55)

1 Give each child a copy of the heart (page 55). Help them to fold the page along the dotted line and hold the fold as they cut out the shape. They should end up with a heart.

2 Read the words on the page together. They remind us that God knows everything about us, so we can talk to him honestly about anything: our families and friends, problems we have, things we wish we hadn't done and things we want to thank God for.

3 Give the children time to write or draw some of those things on the inside of the folded heart. Suggest they chat quietly to God as they do so. They can close their hearts to take home, knowing that God listens to everything they say to him.

Game

 minutes

Why: to remember that we can talk to God about anything at any time
With: music and means to play it

1 Write the numbers 1 to 12 on sheets of paper and arrange them around the room as on a clock. Ask children to stand at 9, 12 and 3 o'clock: the special prayer times at the Temple in Jesus' time. Ask the children if they have a special time to pray. Say that special prayer times are good, but we can pray at other times too.

2 Encourage the children to move around the circle clockwise as the music plays. When it stops, invite them to stand by the nearest number.

3 Ask them to think where they might be at that time of day, who they might be with and what they might be doing. What might they talk to God about at that time? Ask them to remember especially the times when they find things difficult or are tempted to do wrong things. God will be listening!

Craft prayer

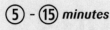 *minutes*

Why: to learn about being sorry
With: copies of page 56 (on card if possible), split pins

1 Teach the children the slogan, 'Don't be smug; be sorry'. Say that it will help them to remember to treat others better than themselves.

2 Give each child a copy of page 56. Help them to cut out the two figures and rods. Encourage them to write 'Don't be smug; be sorry' on the rods. (Give extra help to younger children, if they need it.)

3 Make holes in the card where marked and show the children how to attach the figures to the rods with split pins. Encourage the children to move the figures by pulling and pushing the rods so that the Pharisee can tip forward (arrogant and overpowering) and the tax collector can bow humbly.

4 Encourage the children to take the models home and remember not to be smug, but to ask God to forgive them for the wrong things they do. Remind the children that God loves them very much and wants to be close to them.

Picture for use with **Prayer heart**

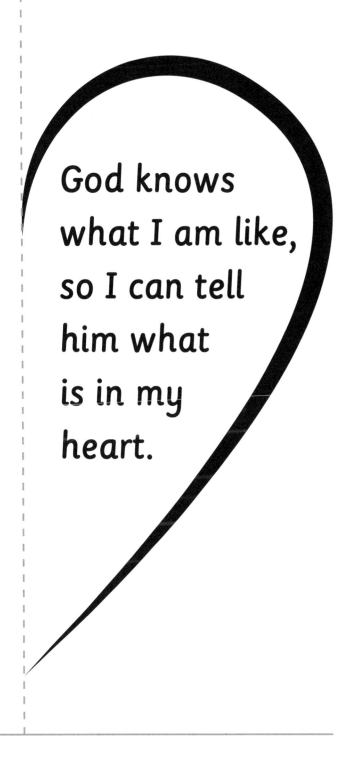

God knows what I am like, so I can tell him what is in my heart.

Fold along the dotted line.
Hold the fold and cut out the shape.
Unfold to find a heart.

Templates for use with **Craft prayer**

EXTENSION IDEAS

Activities for younger children

Ways to pray

 minutes

Why: to enjoy praying in lots of different ways

1 Sing the following song to the tune: 'One man went to mow':
We can talk to God, talk to God together. Let's all pray to God right now, talk to God together.

2 Tell the children you are going to try different ways of 'talking' to God. Sing: We can talk to God, talk to God together. Loudly, loudly, talk to God, talk to God together.

3 Talk to God in that way now, with the children saying their own words.

4 Repeat the song, varying the words in italics, for example, softly, jumping, clapping, standing, sitting, with others, sadly. Follow up each verse with a short prayer time.

5 If the children find it hard to think of what to say to God in a particular style, be ready to supply simple words for them to repeat.

Bible story picture

⑤ - ⑩ *minutes*

Why: to realise that God wants us to be close to him
With: a copy of the picture on page 58 (printed on A4 paper) for each child or enlarged copies for group use, art and craft materials, an adult helper, rugs, cushions, books of prayers, pictures, items for the children to hold such as a small wooden cross, a piece of soft fabric, a favourite cuddly toy

1 You can use the picture as an introduction to the Bible story or to help you review the story together.

2 During each session of this *Mosaic* series about prayer, set out an area of your meeting space as a 'prayer corner'. Make the area comfortable, with cushions and rugs to sit on.

Provide things to look at, admire and handle. Include pictures from the Bible story and art materials to decorate them.

3 Arrange to have a leader available to join any children in the prayer corner, to listen and encourage their exploration and to suggest ways to pray, as appropriate. Keep this low-key, welcoming, unpressured and optional.

For older children

Honesty session

⑤ *minutes*

Why: to discover how we can pray honestly
With: notebooks to give to each child (optional)

1 Share with your group how you pray. Be as honest as you can be about your prayer life (without giving away inappropriate information). If prayer has ever been a challenge for you, this might be a helpful thing to share too.

2 Invite the children to ask you questions. Keep it light-hearted. Don't be afraid to say if you don't know the answer, but try and find out by the next time you meet. You could also ask the children questions about their prayer life!

3 Assure the children that you pray for them (if you do). Remind them that they can always ask you to pray about something, as well as praying about it themselves.

4 Encourage them to keep a prayer diary. This can be a simple sheet of paper or you can encourage children to have an attractive notebook to record their prayers and answers: you might like to consider giving each child a suitable blank book or a resource such as *You and God* (prayer journal by Elaine Carr, for 11–14s, published by Scripture Union @ £5.99 ISBN 978 1 84427 399 7).

THE LEARN AND REMEMBER VERSE

'Don't worry about anything, but in all your prayers ask God for what you need, always asking him with a thankful heart.'

Philippians 4:6

Invite the children to share things that they worry about, things they need and things they want to thank God for. Say the verse together, then take it in turns to pray about the things they have mentioned.

Find a poster for this Learn and remember verse on page 59.

You could also use the song 'Don't worry', on the *Bitesize Bible Songs 2* CD, available from Scripture Union.

Use with
Bible story picture
We can talk and
listen to God!
Luke 18:9–14

Philippians 4:6

'Don't worry about anything, but in all your prayers ask God for what you need, always asking him with a thankful heart.'

Mosaic clinic

Top tips from ministry practitioners to help you make the most of your small group with a wide age range.

BIBLE HELP
Let's be honest – there are no Bible verses that tell us specifically how to lead a mixed-age group. This kind of context simply doesn't feature in the Bible. We do have hints and clues though that our work with this kind of group can be good and can bear fruit.

God-followers together
Imagine the crowds of families of God-followers who for centuries, several times a year, headed for 'the place where the Lord chooses to be worshipped' (Deuteronomy 16:2,6,11,15,16), to celebrate the great Jewish festivals. For instance:

'After you have finished the grain harvest and the grape harvest, take your sons and daughters and all your servants to the place where the LORD chooses to be worshipped. Celebrate the Festival of Shelters for seven days. Also invite the poor, including Levites, foreigners, orphans and widows' (Deuteronomy 16:13–15).

Think about...
To what extent does the following description ring true for your group? 'At times the children and adults will walk along together, talking as they go, sharing stories with first one person and then another, each observing different things and sharing their discoveries. At times the children will lag behind and some of the adults will have to wait for them and urge them on. Sometimes the smallest children may ask to be carried. At other times, though, the children will dash ahead making new discoveries and may, perhaps, pull the adults along to see what they have found' (*Children in the Way*, Church House Publishing, 1988).

....

They all travelled together – toddlers, children, youth, adults and old people – to worship the Lord. This helps us understand how, one Passover, Jesus came to be 'left behind' in Jerusalem, his parents not being sure who he might be travelling with (Luke 2:41–52).

The family model
Bringing up children and young people in the faith was the task of parents supported by the broader faith community (Deuteronomy 6:1–9), and this happened all through the year. This was the best approach, according to God.

In New Testament times all ages met together for worship and learning, usually in homes – there's no suggestion that this was a poor second best approach either. Children, youth and adults grew in

Top Tips on Working with Mixed Ages by Maggie Barfield and Terry Clutterham £3.99

faith by hearing the same things and sharing the same experiences. It was only in the early 1800s that churches decided they could handle things better if children and young people were split into age-specific groups – that they could learn faith in the same way that they learned maths at school! Was this a serious mistake?

Of course God knew how best to nurture faith in children and young people – the emphasis was on families remembering, doing, modelling and learning together. For our mixed-age group, as leaders we're providing help for our group members to grow in faith either because Christian parents need our support in this or because our group members don't have Christian parents. As we work *in loco parentis*, there's no reason why this shouldn't be a great context for the children and young people to get to know God and grow in him.

Shepherds of God's flock

While we can't discover directly from the Bible how to run a mixed-age group, we can find plenty of help with knowing the kind of leader we should be. Let's explore 1 Peter 5 together, verses 2 to 11, which start with the image of Middle Eastern shepherds (verse 2).

Think about...
The life of a shepherd could be very hard and lonely, as Jacob discovered (Genesis 31:40,41). Out in the hills in all kinds of weather, he watched over his sheep, leading them to good pasture, rescuing them from dangerous places, and protecting them from wild animals. Without their shepherd, the sheep were helpless. A good shepherd took his work very seriously; he would risk his life for the sheep if necessary (John 10:11), and would search for even one missing sheep until he found it. (*The Book of Bible Knowledge*, Scripture Union, 1982)

Pause to pray for the 'sheep' in your care, and your 'shepherding' of them.

Remember that the 'flock' is God's, not ours. Our job is to look after it for him. We should be 'shepherds' who: do the job in order to please God, not because we feel we have to – it should be a joy (verse 2b); don't do it for what we can get out of it, but for what we can put into it (verse 2b); are models to our group of what it means to serve God (verse 3); will be richly rewarded for what we do (verse 4).

Think about...
Study these Bible verses with your other leader(s). What can you learn from verses 5 to 11 about yourselves as leaders of your group?

SERIES INTRODUCTION

JESUS, THE FRIEND

God's love and compassion are seen in Jesus' encounters with four individuals.

BIBLE BACKGROUND FOR YOU

One of the things that strikes us about Jesus as we meet him in the Gospels is the way that he always has time for people - and often not the people that we would expect. Our first session has him with someone expected - a religious leader. Despite Nicodemus' difficulty in understanding what Jesus is saying, Jesus is patient and sensitive throughout.

If this is an expected meeting the next is totally unexpected. For a Jewish rabbi to talk to a woman, alone, especially a woman of doubtful reputation, was unheard of. And yet here is Jesus displaying exactly the same respect, sensitivity and patience as he does with Nicodemus.

The next two accounts show Jesus healing rather than talking. But again the key notes are sensitivity and care for the individual. In the case of the official he offers gentle but clear reassurance. In both the power of Jesus is evident as healing occurs. In both the effect is to bring about faith.

We can read these accounts as a reminder of who Jesus is and the way in which he works with people. Do we expect to see Jesus at work in similar ways today? Do we show the same patience and sensitivity to those in our groups, to Christian friends and to non-Christians we know?

For your small group with a wide age range

This series helps us discover God's compassion through stories of people who encountered Jesus and were changed.

These passages from John's Gospel are full of deep meaning, so it is important to keep the session aims in mind and avoid trying to achieve too much, especially with our younger children.

As we 'witness' Jesus teaching, befriending and healing, be bold enough to allow him to speak of God's compassion to each individual.

Resources for ministry

Mega Top Tips on Offering the Best Children's Ministry
Bishop Paul Butler shares practical advice and real-life stories to help you offer the best children's ministry. With ideas on how to build great ministry – in churches, in families, in the wider community and in the world, and biblical insights into how we view and treat all children, this compact book will help you to get to grips with big issues fast.

Highlights from *LightLive*

Go to the 'Search *LightLive*' tab at www.lightlive.org and enter this session's Bible reference to find:

- 'Audio Bible story': a regular mp3 download for 3–7s
- 'Learn and remember': a PowerPoint of a Bible verse to learn, for 5–11s (see also page 95)
- 'Presentation': an activity with animation for 11–14s

SESSION 1
Fresh start

Bible:
John 3:1–21

Aim: To find out that God is keen to answer honest questions about who Jesus is

CORE PROGRAMME

For 3 to 14s

Bible story with questions

 minutes

Why: to find out that God is keen to answer honest questions about who Jesus is
With: SU *Bible Timeline* or the *Big Bible Storybook Timeline* (see page 96 for details), washable pens, stick puppets (page 64) (all optional)

1 *Bible Timeline*
Ask a child to stand next to one of the characters that they know on the *Timeline*. Ask another child to face the opposite direction and try to guess who they are standing next to, by asking questions such as 'Are you a man?' and 'Are you in the Old Testament?'

Explain that today Nicodemus asks Jesus lots of questions to find out more about him.

2 **Bible story**
Invite the children to hold up their index fingers and say that, today, one will be 'Jesus' and the other will be someone called 'Nicodemus'. (You could draw faces on the fingers with washable pens. Or make stick puppets as described in Puppets on page 72.) Encourage the children to copy you as you hold up your Nicodemus finger, at arm's length, and explain that he is at the end of the road. Say that Nicodemus was a very important man who knew a lot about laws and rules. Bring your finger slowly closer, as if he is walking along the road. Explain that it is night-time.

Read John 3:1,2. Ask the children why they think Nicodemus was going out to find Jesus in the middle of the night. What sort of person was Jesus? Why was it important for Nicodemus to go and see Jesus? Give them time to respond.

Hold up your Jesus finger and bring Nicodemus closer to it.

Read their conversation from John 3:2–13, moving the relevant finger as they 'speak'.

Explain that Nicodemus asked Jesus if God had sent him, because he knew that Jesus had done some amazing things that only God could help him with. Jesus explained that to understand all of the things he was doing Nicodemus needed to be born again.

Nicodemus couldn't understand what Jesus had just said: he really didn't know how to be born a second time! Jesus explained that being born again isn't like being born as a small baby, but it is like having a new start with God. God's Spirit gives us the new life when we are born again. We can't see the Spirit but it can really change us from the inside. Nicodemus still didn't understand what Jesus was saying, and Jesus was amazed that even though Nicodemus was such an important teacher he still had to ask lots of questions. He told Nicodemus that he would never understand things that happen in heaven, if he couldn't understand things that happened on earth.

Put your fingers down. Read John 3:14–17. Say that the Bible tells us that God sent Jesus to help others to believe, and that God loves the world so much! For Nicodemus, and for everyone, God sent his only Son so that everyone who believes in him will never die but will live for ever with him.

3 **Chat**
Ask the children why they think Nicodemus had to ask all of those questions. Ask them if they ever have questions about Jesus, about the Bible or about their own lives. Give them time to respond. Thank God together that he is keen to answer our questions any time of the night or day.

For use with **Bible story with questions**

CORE PROGRAMME CONTINUED

Praising God

 minutes

Why: to realise that God reveals himself
With: a selection of leaves, pressed flowers and twigs, or pictures (pages 66 and 67)

1 Invite each child to choose a leaf, a pressed flower or a twig (or use the pictures from pages 66 and 67). Say that, in his creation, God shows us what he is like.

2 Ask the children to look at their object and think about what God shows us about himself in it. (For instance: he loves colour; he makes everything different.)

3 Take it in turns to say a short prayer to tell God how great he is, based on the things the children have come up with. For example, 'Thank you, God, that you want us to know that you love colours, just like the colours in this leaf.'

Being sorry

 minutes

Why: to say 'sorry' and make a fresh start
With: *Reach Up!* CD, available from Scripture Union, and means to play it, a large sheet of paper, pencils, erasers, sheet music and lyrics for 'When you make a mistake' (pages 68 and 69)

1 Explain that, in today's story, Nicodemus learns how to make a fresh start with God. Say that we can make a fresh start, too, and give each child a pencil.

2 Play 'When you make a mistake' from the *Reach Up!* CD. Ask the children to write or draw things that they are sorry for on the large sheet of paper. Then ask them to take it in turns to rub out their word or picture and thank God that we can start all over again whenever we need to.

Team game

 minutes

Why: to think about who Jesus is
With: questions and answers for 'Team game' (pages 70 and 71)

1 In advance, print out and cut up two copies of the questions and answers (available on pages 70 and 71).

2 Put your group into two teams. Invite the teams to line up at one end of the room. Give the teams the questions about Jesus and place the answers at the opposite end of the room.

3 Explain to the children that they must run to the other end of the room one by one, collecting an answer each time, and then fit the correct questions and answers together. The first team to complete this wins. The pictures and puzzle-piece style should aid your non-readers.

4 After the game, talk about the questions about Jesus.

Pictures for use with **Praising God**

Pictures for use with **Praising God**

Music for use with **Being sorry**

When you make a mistake

Leanne Mitchell

Lyric sheet for use with **Being sorry**

When you make a mistake

Leanne Mitchell

When you make a mistake – don't worry,

God will wipe away wrong – say sorry.

God is a loving God and he forgives.

God is a loving God

And he wants you to live.

God is powerful, God is great!

He's with you ev'ry day.

God is wonderful, God is love,

And he forgives – in ev'ry way.

Pictures for use with **Team game**

Pictures for use with **Team game**

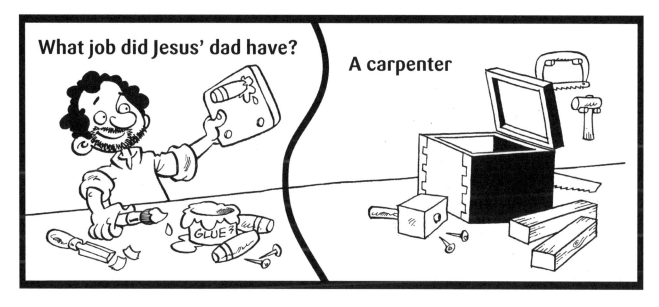

EXTENSION IDEAS

Activities for younger children

Puppets

 minutes

Why: to ask Jesus our honest questions
With: puppets and scenery (page 64), spare pencils

1 Explain that when Nicodemus asked Jesus questions he found out who Jesus was.

2 Give each child a copy of the puppets (page 64) and invite them to cut out and colour the two characters. Help them to tape the Nicodemus puppet to a pencil and do the same for the Jesus puppet. Cut along the line down the middle of the road for them.

3 Suggest the children draw themselves and stick their picture on a pencil, too.

4 Encourage them to work in pairs to play with the puppets, with one child bringing the puppet of Nicodemus along the road to meet Jesus and ask him questions, and the other child's Jesus puppet answering. Then let them use their puppets of themselves to chat with Jesus, too.

Bible story picture

 minutes

Why: to explore ways of 'visiting' Jesus
With: a copy of the picture on page 73 (printed on A4 paper) for each child or enlarged copies for group use, art and craft materials

1 You can use the picture as an introduction to the Bible story or to help you review the story together.

2 Show the children the Bible story picture and guide them to identify one of the characters as Jesus. Who could the other person be? What does he look like? Comment on his clothes and the little box on his headband that has words from the Bible inside. Do the children think he looks important?

3 Introduce the second character as Nicodemus and agree that he was an important man. He wanted to talk to Jesus but he did not want other people to know, so he came to see Jesus at night. How could the children make their pictures look like night-time ones? Help them to think about colours, lights and shadows, before completing their pictures.

For older children

Collage

 minutes

Why: to think about people's questions about Jesus
With: newspapers, magazines, a large sheet of paper

1 Ask the children to suggest questions other people might have about Jesus. Write them down as they say them.

2 Using pictures from newspapers and magazines, make a collage with lots of different sorts of people clustered around a cross. Invite the children to draw speech bubbles from their mouths with the questions they thought of earlier inside them.

3 As they make their collage, ask the children to think of ways of answering other people's questions about God. Say that when we know the truth about Jesus, he may use us to help other people find the answers to their questions about him.

4 Pray that we will be happy to answer other people's questions about Jesus.

THE LEARN AND REMEMBER VERSE

'Listen! I stand at the door and knock; if anyone hears my voice and opens the door, I will come in and eat with them, and they will eat with me.'

Revelation 3:20

Repeat the verse with actions for key words: listen, stand, knock, hear, open, eat, with me.

Find a poster for this Learn and remember verse on page 95.

You could also use the song 'Listen', on the *Bitesize Bible Songs 2* CD, available from Scripture Union.

Use with **Bible story picture**
An evening visitor John 3:1–21

SESSION 2

No secrets

Bible:
John 4:3–42

Aim: To discover that God knows all about us and still loves us

CORE PROGRAMME

For 3 to 14s

Bible story with model

(20) minutes

Why: to discover that God knows all about us and still loves us
With: SU *Bible Timeline* or the *Big Bible Storybook Timeline* (optional, see page 96 for details), 'Guess who' pictures (enlarged and copied from pages 76 and 77), chairs or tables, old sheets, masking tape, story pictures for 'Bible story with model' (page 75), string, plastic cups, a bucket of water, blue powder paint, a white crayon, a paintbrush, the *Reach Up!* CD (available from Scripture Union) and means to play it

1 Set up

Make a well in your meeting area – either with chairs in a small circle facing outwards and covered in old sheets, or by taping a square or circular shape to the floor. Stick each picture (available on page 75) to a plastic cup with a string attached, and placed down the 'well'. Make sure that the string is long enough to hang out of your 'well' so the children can pretend to draw water by pulling up the cups with the string.

2 Guess who?

Gradually reveal your 'Guess who' pictures (if possible, enlarged from pages 76 and 77), to identify aspects of a Bible character's life from the SU *Bible Timeline*. For example, show pictures of a sheep, harp, sling, crown and arrows to help the children guess 'David'. When they have guessed the identity of the person, they need to explain how the pictures represent part of the character's life. Play this for David and/or Moses.

3 Story with the well

Read John 4:3–19,25–33,39–42 to the children from a child-friendly version, such as the CEV. When you get to the verses listed below, stop and ask a child to pull up a cup from the well to see if it has the right picture to illustrate this part of the story. If not, ask them to let their cup down again. When they have found the right cup, place it in a line outside the well.

Verses 4,5: Find the picture of Jesus walking into Samaria.

Verses 6–8: Find the picture of the disciples walking off to town and the picture of Jesus sitting by the well. (Two cups.)

Verse 10: Find the picture of Jesus talking to the Samaritan woman.

Verse 15: Find the picture of the woman begging Jesus to give her a drink of his life-giving water.

Verse 18: Find the picture of Jesus telling the woman about her five husbands.

Verse 26: Find the picture of Jesus telling the woman that he is the Messiah.

Verse 27: Find the picture of the disciples returning.

Verse 28: Find the picture of the woman leaving her water jug and running off.

Verses 33: Find the picture of the disciples trying to get Jesus to eat something.

Verses 39–42: Find the picture of many people putting their faith in Jesus.

4 Reflect

Ask the children to think how the woman must have felt, knowing that Jesus knew everything about her. Ask the children if they think God still loved her. Give them time to respond. Explain that even though we cannot see God, he knows everything about us, and he loves us very much.

Pictures for use with **Bible story with model**

Cut each picture out and stick each one
on to a plastic cup

Pictures for use with **Bible story with model**
Guess who David pictures

Pictures for use with **Bible story with model**
Guess who Moses pictures

CORE PROGRAMME CONTINUED

5 Recap the story

When they have finished finding all of the pictures, ask the group to retell the story using the cups that are lined up.

Think and draw

 minutes

Why: to think about God loving us at all times in our lives
With: a happy face and a sad face (page 79, enlarged if you wish)

1 Stick up the happy face and sad face. Give each child some sticky notes and invite them to draw a picture of a time when they have been really good. Encourage them to stick their picture next to the happy face.

2 Ask them to draw a picture of a time when they have done something they shouldn't have done, and stick that next to the sad face.

3 Ask the children if God knows about these things. *(Point to the happy and sad face.)* Do they think God loved them when they were doing good things? And bad things? Chat about how God does not love the bad things we do, but that he loves us all the time.

Freeze frames

 minutes

Why: to thank God that he knows everything we do

1 Ask the children to act out something that they do every day. Explain to them that when you shout 'Freeze!', they need to freeze in the position they are in, like a statue. While they are frozen, try to guess what the children are doing and ask them to guess each other's activity.

2 Play again, using different activities.

3 Explain to the children that God knows everything that they do every day. Play the game again, but when you say 'freeze', get everyone to shout, 'Thank you, God, that you know everything we do!'

Finger printing

 minutes

Why: to thank God for knowing everything about us
With: an ink stamp pad

1 Give each child a sheet of white paper and have the ink stamp pad central. Ask the children to make a fingerprint on their paper. Challenge them to compare prints and find someone's fingerprint that is exactly the same as theirs. (They will discover that everybody has different prints.) Say that everyone in the world has a unique fingerprint, and God knows all of them!

2 Invite the children to turn their fingerprints into a picture of themselves, either by adding more prints or by drawing features with pens. As they do this, say that God knows all about us, not just our fingerprints.

Faces for use with **Think and draw**

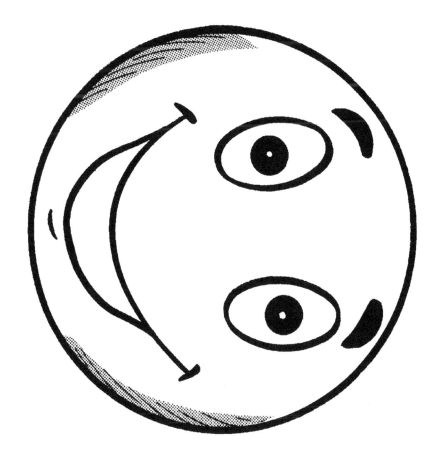

EXTENSION IDEAS

Activities for younger children

Kim's game

 minutes

Why: to learn that Jesus knows and remembers everything about us
With: a tray, a cloth, a collection of various personal items

1 Before the session collect together about five to eight of your own personal items such as your keys, a photo, a handkerchief, a watch or a ring.

2 Show the items, one at a time, and talk about each of them. If you are married you might say that your wedding ring reminds you of how much your wife or husband loves you. Jesus knows this. The keys make you think about your home. Jesus knows where you live, and so on. Place the items one by one on a tray.

3 Let the children add their own items to the tray. Perhaps they have a toy or a hair bobble or some glasses that they could talk about. Jesus knows about these things too.

4 Cover the items up and see how many the children can remember. Even if they forget one of them, Jesus will never forget. He knows and remembers everything about us and loves us completely.

Bible story picture

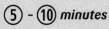 **minutes**

Why: to realise that Jesus knows everything about us
With: a copy of the picture on page 81 (printed on A4 paper) for each child or enlarged copies for group use, art and craft materials

1 You can use the picture as an introduction to the Bible story or to help you review the story together.

2 Look at the Bible story picture together and identify which character is Jesus. Say that the Bible does not tell us the name of the woman in the picture, just that she came from a country called Samaria.

3 Point to the stones and explain that they are making a wall around a 'well', a deep hole in the ground with water at the bottom. Explain that this is how people got water to drink, when there were no taps or bottled water.

4 Listen to the Bible story to find out what Jesus and the woman talked about.

For older children

Praying for nations

⑩ **minutes**

Why: to pray for God's Word to spread
With: map from page 82 for each person

1 Ask someone to read John 4:35,38. Challenge the children to tell you what Jesus means here.

2 Say that, like the Samaritan woman, when we receive God's love we should want to share it.

3 Distribute copies of the map of the world from page 82 and see how many people don't have access to Bibles. Explain that Christians are trying to bring the Bible to everyone in their own language so that all people, everywhere, can learn that Jesus loves them.

4 Ask the children to choose an area where the Bible isn't available and to pray for the people in that place and for the Christians working there.

THE LEARN AND REMEMBER VERSE

'Listen! I stand at the door and knock; if anyone hears my voice and opens the door, I will come in and eat with them, and they will eat with me.'

Revelation 3:20

Challenge the children to draw a picture to illustrate this verse. They can use the picture as a memory aid during the week.

Find a poster for this Learn and remember verse on page 95.

You could also use the song 'Listen', on the *Bitesize Bible Songs 2* CD, available from Scripture Union.

Use with **Bible story picture**
The woman at a well John 4:3-42

Map for use with **Praying for nations**

All over the world there are people who haven't got the Bible in their own language. Wycliffe Bible Translators, who translate the Bible into new languages, say that there are 2,078 languages that the Bible hasn't been translated into yet!

They are aiming that by the year 2025 a Bible translation project will be in progress for every people group that needs it. Will you help them by praying for their work?

The map shows the different areas in the world that need Bible translations

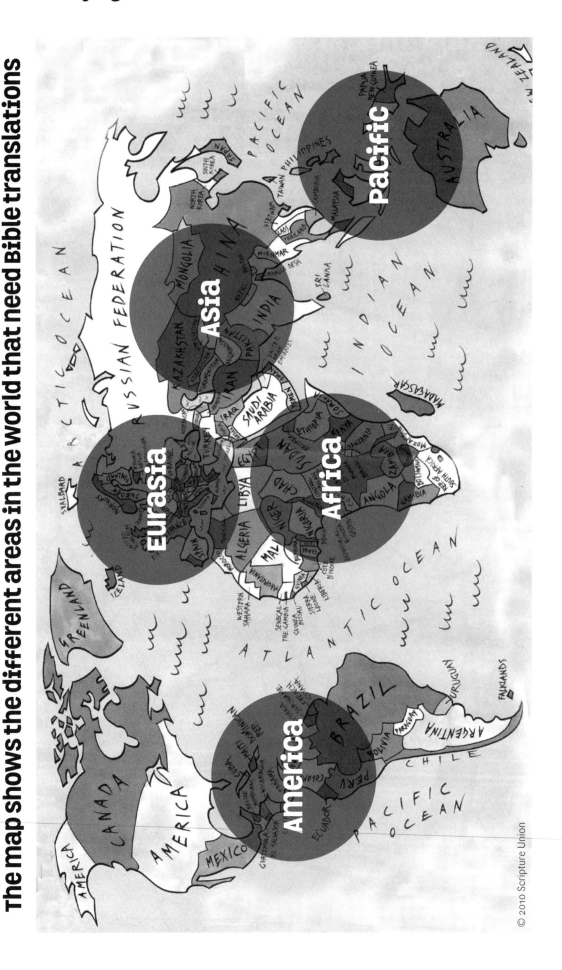

SERIES 3 JESUS, THE FRIEND
SESSION 3
Healing word

Bible:
John 4:43–54

Aim: To see how, through Jesus, people are able to experience God's compassion

CORE PROGRAMME

For 3 to 14s

Bible story with pictures

(20) minutes

Why: to see how, through Jesus, people are able to experience God's compassion
With: enlarged copies of page 84, SU *Bible Timeline* or the *Big Bible Storybook Timeline* (see page 96 for details)

1 Prepare
If possible, make enlarged copies of the pictures on page 84 and cut them out. Put them in order, then write the letters of the word 'COMPASSION' on the back of the pictures, starting with 'C' on picture 1, and so on.

2 Watch and listen
Share out the pictures, and challenge the children to look at their picture and put it at the front when that incident happens in the story. The asterisks (✱) show where to pause and show a picture. (The correct order is as displayed on page 84, reading across the columns.)

Story: When Jesus had spent enough time in Samaria, he decided that he would walk back to Galilee ✱ and spend some time talking to the people there about the love of God.

When he arrived there the people welcomed him ✱ because they had seen all the things that he had done at the Passover feast in Jerusalem, including turning the tables over in the Temple and performing many miracles. They knew that he had lots of exciting things to tell them and they were eager to listen!

Jesus decided to travel to Cana, where he had turned water into wine ✱. He was met by an official who begged Jesus for help. ✱ He told Jesus that his son was very sick. ✱ He knew that Jesus had performed many miracles and that he could heal his son, so he had decided to come to Jesus and beg for his son to be made well again.

The official was very worried because his son was almost dead, but he knew that Jesus could heal him and had decided that going to Cana and finding Jesus may be his son's last chance. Jesus saw the man and had compassion on him. He saw how sad the man was and he wanted to help him.

Jesus said to the man, 'Go, your son will live.' ✱

At once the official believed what Jesus said and ran all the way home to see his son. ✱ He was so excited because he knew how powerful Jesus was and he knew that his son was going to be OK!

On the way home the man met his servants, who were running to meet him ✱ and tell him that his son was well – but of course he already knew!

When he got home, his son was out of bed, ✱ completely better. Jesus had healed him!

From that day forward the official and his household decided that they were going to believe in Jesus ✱ and tell other people about his compassion – about how he cares for people and helps them.

3 Recap
Challenge the children to make sure they have all the pictures and that they are in the right order. Then ask for volunteers to retell the story using their pictures. As they tell the story, turn over the pictures at the appropriate part. When they have finished, the word 'COMPASSION' should be showing.

4 Chat
Ask the children to remember what the word 'compassion' means (to care a lot about someone who is suffering and to want to do something for them; younger

Pictures for use with **Bible story with pictures**

CORE PROGRAMME CONTINUED

children may understand the concept more easily if it is described as 'kindness'). Encourage them to say how they think Jesus showed compassion.

Find out what the children think about Jesus' compassion. Was it real? What does it tell us about God? Are there other examples they can remember or find on the *Bible Timeline*?

Is there something they'd like to say to God about his compassion? If there is, spend a few moments together talking silently to God.

Prayer

 minutes

Why: to pray with compassion (kindness)

1 Ask the children to think of someone who is having a difficult time at the moment. Encourage them to imagine how this person feels, then describe how they feel about this person. Do they want to help them? Explain that just as the official went to Jesus to get help for his son, we can go to Jesus in prayer and ask him to help people. By doing this we are acting compassionately (kindly), and we can also ask God to show his compassion (kindness) to them.

2 Invite the children to pray simple prayers to God, asking him to show compassion to the people they have mentioned. Encourage them to be specific in what they ask God to do, just as the official went to Jesus with a specific request.

Feel

 **minutes**

Why: to think about how we feel about others
With: pictures of people in difficult situations from newspapers or charity magazines such as TEARFund or World Vision

1 Put the pictures out around the room, each with sticky notes and pens near it.

2 Invite the children to walk around silently, choose one picture to look at and think about how they feel about the people in the picture. Encourage them to write a word or draw a small picture on a sticky note and fix it on the picture to describe how they honestly feel about those people. They should then move on to a new picture.

3 Chat about the words they wrote or pictures they made, asking how they think God feels too.

4 Pray, asking God to help us to feel as he does about other people.

Role play

 minutes

Why: to plan to show God's compassion
With: pictures for 'Role play' (page 86)

1 Ask the children to get into pairs. Give each pair one set of the pictures. Challenge each pair to choose one compassionate thing they would like to do this week to show someone that God loves and cares for them. (You may need to ask or remind them what this means, especially if you haven't done 'Sorting game', which helps to explore this concept.) Younger children may find the word 'kindness' easier to understand.

2 Challenge the children to role play the action they have decided to do, taking it in turns to be the person who is being compassionate.

3 The children may like to show each other, or other groups, their act.

4 Finish by asking God to help them to remember to do the compassionate things they have planned to do this week.

Pictures for use with **Role play** and **Sorting game**

EXTENSION IDEAS

Activities for younger children

Sorting game

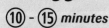 minutes

Why: to introduce the concept of compassion
With: pictures for 'Sorting game' (page 86)

1 Find out from the children what they think the word 'compassionate' might mean. Affirm their ideas. Explain that it means to be caring, kind, loving and concerned for people. Ask the children if they know anyone who is like this. Give them a moment to describe what this person is like.

2 Give each child a set of the pictures for 'Sorting game' (page 86) and challenge them to put them into two piles – one for those pictures where someone is being compassionate, and one where they are not.

3 Say that today they are going to see Jesus doing something compassionate.

Bible story picture

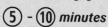 minutes

Why: to recognise that Jesus is able to help and heal people
With: a copy of the picture on page 88 (printed on A4 paper) for each child or enlarged copies for group use, art and craft materials

1 You can use the picture as an introduction to the Bible story or to help you review the story together.

2 Look at the Bible story picture and see if you can find Jesus. 'Realise' that he is not there! Explain that Jesus did something very wonderful for the people in this family – but he did it without even going to see them!

3 Find the boy: explain that he was very ill. Find the dad: say that he went a long way to see Jesus to ask him to make his boy well again. The mum stayed with the boy to look after him because he was very ill. Jesus sent the dad back home *(pause to colour in the dad)*. When he got there, his son was well *(pause to colour the boy)* and everyone was happy *(colour the mum)*.

4 What do the children think about Jesus?

For older children

Acrostic

 minutes

Why: to explore what compassion is
With: a large sheet of paper (optional)

1 Write the word 'COMPASSION' vertically and ask if anyone knows what it means.

2 Say that the dictionary defines compassion as 'a strong feeling of sympathy and sadness for the suffering of others and a desire to help them' (*Cambridge Advanced Learner's Dictionary*).

3 Challenge the children to devise an acrostic for the word 'COMPASSION'. (For example, 'C' could stand for 'Caring for others', 'O' for 'Offering help to others', and so on.) They could do this all together, or in small groups. If done in small groups, allow them to share their acrostics with each other.

THE LEARN AND REMEMBER VERSE

'Listen! I stand at the door and knock; if anyone hears my voice and opens the door, I will come in and eat with them, and they will eat with me.'

Revelation 3:20

Sit with the group round a table eating snacks. (Remember hygiene and allergy issues.) Invite the children to take it in turns to go to the door and say the verse, doing actions of knocking on the door, opening it and then sitting down to eat snacks as they say the relevant words.

Find a poster for this Learn and remember verse on page 95.

You could also use the song 'Listen', on the *Bitesize Bible Songs 2* CD, available from Scripture Union.

Use with **Bible story picture**
A man in need John 4:43–54

SESSION 4
Helping hand

Bible:
John 5:1–18

Aim: To understand how, through Jesus, God brings life

CORE PROGRAMME

For 3 to 14s

Imagine

 minutes

Why: to understand how, through Jesus, God brings life
With: a mat or jumper for each child, story text from page 90 (optional), SU *Bible Timeline* or the *Big Bible Storybook Timeline* (see page 96 for details)

1 Imagine and mime

Begin by looking at the *Bible Timeline* together, and seeing if the children can work out when the story took place. It is one of Jesus' 'miracles of healing', where he helped a man who could not walk.

Give everyone a mat or a jumper. Ask all the children to lie down on their mat or jumper with their eyes closed to imagine the story.

Story: Imagine you cannot walk. You have never been able to walk. You have always had to be carried everywhere, as there are no wheelchairs.

When your friends were learning to walk, you just lay on your mat. When your friends were playing outside, you were lying on your mat. When your friends were out getting jobs and earning money, you were on your mat.

Today you are on your mat by a pool. This pool is special. You've heard that if you get in it when the water moves, you will be able to walk again. The water is moving! You get up on your elbows, but there is no one to help you – and someone else gets in.

The water stops. You are still on your mat. How do you feel? *(Allow the children to respond, and then go back to lying still with their eyes closed.)*

You are on your mat, and a man comes and asks you if you want to get well. How do you feel? *(Allow the children to respond, and then go back to lying still with their eyes closed. Say that they should listen and do what the man says in this part of the story.)*

The man tells you to pick up your mat and walk. Immediately, you can feel a change in your legs. There is strength there you have never felt before. You lift up one leg. *(Pause for the children to do this.)* Then you move your other leg. *(Pause for the children to do this.)* Then you get up and roll up your mat. *(Pause*

for the children to do this.) You walk around. *(Pause for the children to do this.)* You walk and you walk and you walk. How do you feel? *(Allow the children to respond, and then carry on walking.)* You are walking and walking.

Some important religious men come and tell you it is wrong for you to be carrying your mat because it is the day of rest. How do you feel? *(Allow the children to respond.)*

You say that the man who healed you told you to pick up your mat and walk. They ask who healed you, but you don't know, so you carry on walking. *(The children start walking again.)*

You walk to the Temple. In the Temple, the man who healed you comes up to you again and tells you not to sin, but just to do things which please God. How do you feel?

2 Discuss

Ask what two changes Jesus made in the man's life. *(He healed him; and he told him not to sin.)* Encourage the children to tell you what they think sin is. *(Things that we do that don't please God.)*

Explain that not sinning means we are pleasing God. This is the life God wants all of us to have – life to the full; real life that goes on for ever – because if we live to please God, we will live with him for ever.

Script for use with **Imagine**

Imagine you cannot walk. You have never been able to walk. You have always had to be carried everywhere, as there are no wheelchairs. When your friends were learning to walk, you just lay on your mat. When your friends were playing outside, you were lying on your mat. When your friends were out getting jobs and earning money, you were on your mat. Today you are on your mat by a pool. This pool is special. You've heard that if you get in it when the water moves, you will be able to walk again. The water is moving! You get up on your elbows, but there is no one to help you – and someone else gets in. The water stops. You are still on your mat. How do you feel?

(Allow the children to respond, and then go back to lying still with their eyes closed.)

You are on your mat, and a man comes and asks you if you want to get well. How do you feel?

(Allow the children to respond, and then go back to lying still with their eyes closed. Say that they should listen and do what the man says in this part of the story.)

The man tells you to pick up your mat and walk.

Immediately, you can feel a change in your legs. There is strength there you have never felt before. You lift up one leg. *(Pause for the children to do this.)* Then you move your other leg. *(Pause for the children to do this.)* Then you get up and roll up your mat. *(Pause for the children to do this.)* You walk around. *(Pause for the children to do this.)* You walk and you walk and you walk. How do you feel?

(Allow the children to respond, and then carry on walking.)

You are walking and walking. Some important religious men come and tell you it is wrong for you to be carrying your mat because it is the day of rest. How do you feel?

(Allow the children to respond.)

You say that the man who healed you told you to pick up your mat and walk. They ask who healed you, but you don't know, so you carry on walking.

(The children start walking again.)

You walk to the Temple. In the Temple, the man who healed you comes up to you again and tells you not to sin, but just to do things which please God. How do you feel?

CORE PROGRAMME CONTINUED

Challenge the children to compare having your legs healed and being able to live with God for ever. Both are good options but do they think one is better than the other? Encourage them to explain the reasons for their choices.

Prayer

 -  *minutes*

Why: to pray for help and healing for sick friends and family

1 Encourage the children to think of some people they know who are sick or need help in their lives, like the way man in the story needed and received help from Jesus.

2 Invite them to take it in turns to pray simple prayers, asking Jesus to do things to bring life to the people they've talked about. Help them to be as specific as possible.

Forgiveness

 -  *minutes*

Why: to think about walking with God
With: a rucksack full of heavy objects

1 Challenge the children to remind you what Jesus did for and said to the man. (*He fixed his legs and told him not to sin so he could 'walk with God'.*) Ask them what they think 'sin' is. (*Walking away from God.*) Liken 'sins' to heavy objects in a rucksack (let one or two try lifting the bag), which make it harder for us to walk with God.

2 Ask the children to think of things they did last week that didn't please God. Explain that, when we are sorry, God forgives us. It's as if the weights are taken out of the rucksack so we can walk comfortably with God again.

3 Invite the children to say sorry to God, taking an object out of the rucksack as they do so. Feel the difference!

Prayer collage

 minutes

Why: to pray for friends and families to know that Jesus gives life
With: a large sheet of paper

1 Challenge the children to think of people they want to pray for, who need to know Jesus and the life he brings: friends, family, people in the news or people in other countries who have not heard about Jesus.

2 Invite them to draw round their hands, cut out the hand shape and write the person's name on it, or they could write one name on each finger on the hand shape. Make a collage tree, drawing the outline of a trunk and branches, and using the hand shapes as leaves.

3 Invite the children to come and touch the outline of their hand and, as they do so, to ask God to touch that person's life.

EXTENSION IDEAS
Activities for younger children

Making puppets

 minutes

Why: to enjoy and express the man's response to Jesus
With: page 93, card, scissors, crayons, sharp scissors or a craft knife for adult use only

1 Photocopy page 93 on to card. Help the children to cut around the outlines (or you could do this for the children before the session). Let the children colour in the people. You will need to cut out the two finger-holes on each puppet. Let the children put their fingers through the holes to make legs for the puppets.

2 Let the children act out the Bible story to each other, with the puppets. Make the man puppet lie down and then jump up and down and dance when he is healed.

3 Pray together, thanking Jesus for making people better. You could make your puppet dance along to a praise song.

Bible story picture

 minutes

Why: to respond to Jesus, the Son of God
With: a copy of the picture on page 94 (printed on A4 paper) for each child or enlarged copies for group use, art and craft materials

1 You can use the picture as an introduction to the Bible story or to help you review the story together.

2 Find Jesus in the Bible story picture. Who else is in the scene? Describe what the man is doing. (Standing and carrying a blanket or 'bed'.) Do the children think the man looks well or poorly? Is he happy or sad?

3 While the children complete their pictures, explain that this picture shows the very end of the story. At the start of the story, the man was not very happy and could not walk. Now something has happened: can the children suggest what it could be?

4 Ask the children how they might have felt to be the man in the story. What might they have thought about Jesus?

For older children

Chat

 **⑤ – ⑩** *minutes*

Why: to explore physical, emotional and spiritual healing

1 Help everyone to look up and read John 5:1–7 from the Good News Bible or Contemporary English Version.

2 Ask the children what the man needed. Draw their attention to verse 7. Draw out how the man needed healing for his body, but also for his mind and his spirit.

3 Encourage the children with the knowledge that Jesus can heal all of us – our bodies, minds and spirits. Make sure you allow time to ask Jesus for these kinds of healing after the story.

THE LEARN AND REMEMBER VERSE

'Listen! I stand at the door and knock; if anyone hears my voice and opens the door, I will come in and eat with them, and they will eat with me.'

Revelation 3:20

See who can remember the verse, using the actions or pictures from previous sessions. Ask what they found most helpful to remember the verse. Help them find the verse in a Bible, to discover who is saying the words and what is said before and afterwards.

Find a poster for this Learn and remember verse on page 95.

You could also use the song 'Listen', on the *Bitesize Bible Songs 2* CD, available from Scripture Union.

Templates for use with **Making puppets**

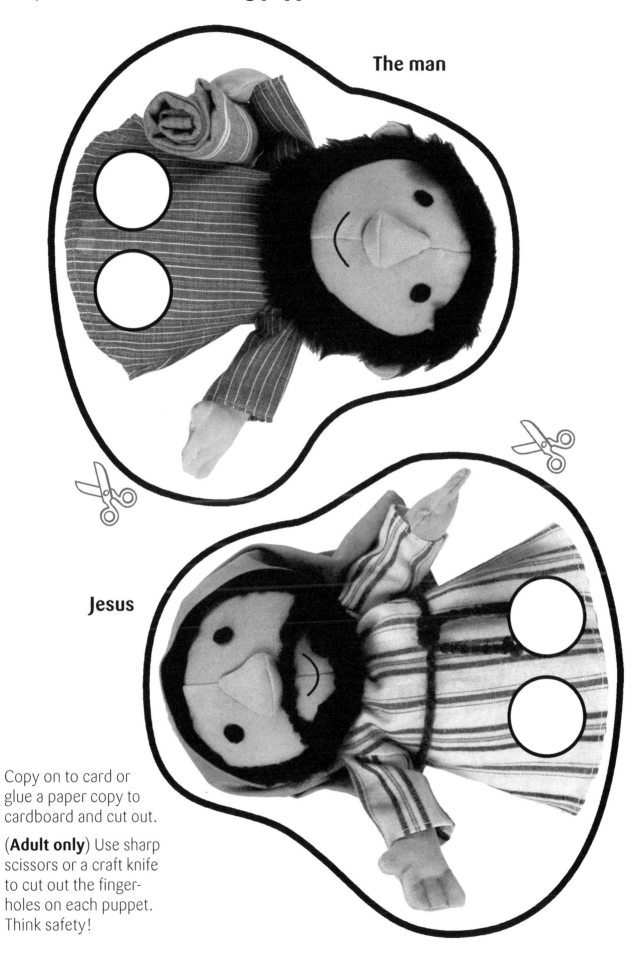

The man

Jesus

Copy on to card or
glue a paper copy to
cardboard and cut out.

(**Adult only**) Use sharp
scissors or a craft knife
to cut out the finger-
holes on each puppet.
Think safety!

Use with **Bible story picture**
A man by a pool John 5:1–18

'Listen! I stand at the door and knock; if anyone hears my voice and opens the door, I will come in and eat with them, and they will eat with me.'

Revelation 3:20

MOSAIC BOOKSHELF

Scripture Union's *Bible Timelines* have helped thousands of children get to know the big story of the Bible - God's great plan for salvation - for many years now. Each colourful and informative version (for young children, older children and young people) takes you through the big story of the Bible from Creation to Revelation, in 16 illustrated panels. Choose one, or more, to introduce the children in your small group to God's big picture.

The Big Bible Storybook Timeline

£11.99 ISBN 978 1 84427 361 4

Does the story of Moses come before or after David, in the Bible? Was Paul around at the same time as Jesus? For most of us, Bible reading, teaching or sermons happen piecemeal – a verse here, a chapter there, maybe a complete letter or a short book. The *Big Bible Storybook*

Timeline is here to help you see God's big story in its historical order.

The pack contains the four-part illustrated *Big Bible Storybook Timeline* poster with adhesive strips, ready to be joined together, together with suggestions for activities to use with children.

Through the Bible
Youth Timeline – A Bible Timeline for Young People (new and updated version)

£11.99 ISBN 978 1 84427 644 8

To young people, the Bible can appear dull, complicated or irrelevant. *Through the Bible* sets out to dispel those preconceptions. This timeline helps young people and their leaders discover more about some of the main characters in the

Bible, and build their understanding of the big themes, such as sin, covenant and prophecy. These themes form a framework on which young people can hang the individual stories they encounter.

Made of four separate pieces, the timeline can be joined together into one long poster to be displayed in a church or youth group setting; or kept in its folder and brought out when needed, if display facilities are limited.

Bible Timeline
(new and updated version)

£11.99 ISBN 978 1 84427 643 1

What's the big story all about? Scripture Union's *Bible Timeline* will help you answer this question, at a glance. The 16 panels each illustrate a key person or event in Bible history. Underneath each picture, key dates and characters are highlighted. Bible references will help you locate the stories in the Bible quickly and easily.

The pack contains the four-part illustrated *Bible Timeline* poster with adhesive strips, ready to be joined together, together with ideas to help you make the most of your *Bible Timeline*.

Mini Bible Timeline

75p ISBN 978 1 84427 729 2

This new *Mini Bible Timeline* has been produced to complement its larger counterpart. The story of the Old Testament appears on one side of this fold-up pocket guide, while the New Testament story is on the other. Using engaging artwork and text, this retelling of the Bible story will be useful for leaders and makes a great gift for the children in your group.

Mini Bible Timeline (10 pack)

£4.99 ISBN 978 1 84427 730 8

This multi-buy offer makes the *Mini Bible Timeline* even more affordable. Why not buy a set and give one to each child in your group?